Published by

Rick Baker

Ken Miller

Design and Layout
Ken Miller

Contributors
Simon Pritchard, Justyn Hughes, Darren Wheeling, Brett Ratner, Hamma Horra, Toby Russell

Special Thanks to
Eihi Shiina, Moon Lee, Brett Ratner, Mark Duffield, Tim Hollingsworth, Toby Russell

Printing
IngramSpark

All rights reserved. No part of this publication may be reproduced or transmitted by any means, graphic, electronic or mechanical, including photocopying, recording, taping or any information storage and retrieval system, without prior written permission of the publishers. Copyright Eastern Heroes.

Cover Illustration
Darren Wheeling

EASTERN HEROES FILM FRENZY

Hi everyone! Welcome to the first, fantastic issue of *Film Frenzy*, which is *Eastern Heroes* magazine's new companion publication. Here we will be focusing on Asian horror, fantasy, science fiction and cult movies.

The main thread for this inaugural issue is definitely the ongoing appreciation of foxy, fast-fighting sci-fi film femme fatales. Interviews with Eihi Shiina and Moon Lee, as well as a large retrospective on Sally Yeh, remind us that Asian cinema knows how to create interesting, tough-cookie women characters. The simply fabulous cover artwork by Darren Wheeling and a feature on some key she-powered science fiction actioners, like *The Heroic Trio* and *Silver Hawk*, do their bit to enhance this issue's main theme.

There's a lot more to enjoy here, such as tons of movie reviews, including a whole section devoted to Chinese creature features. Hollywood uber-director Brett Ratner fills us in on how he first met Jackie Chan and explains why he's decided to publish the upcoming *New Essential Guide to Hong Kong Movies* (which is going to include loads of horror & fantasy films), there's a large horror flicks poster gallery, Mark Duffield recalls what it was like to direct the creepy Thai supernatural chiller *Ghost of Mae Nak*, and, somehow, an article looking at those pesky hopping vampire films is also jammed inside here.

Please enjoy!
Ken Miller
Editor

CONTENTS

04 - AN ARTISTIC GORE GIRL
Eihi Shiina talks about her movies and how she loves to create her own art.

14 - HOPPING MADNESS!
A look at how actor Lam Ching-Ying led the craze in hopping vampire films.

18 - GRACE AND GRIT
A swift and sweet chat with **Moon Lee**, star of the *Angel* girls-with-guns films.

21 - BRETT RATNER ON JACKIE CHAN
Director **Brett Ratner** talks about Jackie Chan and a new Hong Kong film guide.

24 - FILM FRENZY REVIEWS
Reviews of Asian sci-fi, horror & fantasy flicks, both old and new.

36 - SUCCESS HER WAY
Actress and singer Sally Yeh's fruitful career is delved into and remembered.

44 - REIMAGINING A THAI LEGEND
British director **Mark Duffield** on making a movie about a legendary Thai ghost.

54 - BEASTS FROM THE EAST
Tons of Chinese monster movies are reviewed. One features mutant barnacles!

68 - FEARLESS FEMME FIGHTERS OF THE FANTASTIC
A dive into such fun furious-femmes flicks as *I Love Maria* and *The Heroic Trio*.

78 - HORROR FILMS POSTER GALLERY
Drool over some great horror posters from the 80s and early 90s.

EIHI SHIINA

Interviewed by Simon Pritchard

AN ARTISTIC GORE GIRL

Eihi Shiina is an actor, model, poet, photographer and art director. She is best known for her exquisitely delicate, yet brutal, role in *Audition*. Her other roles include Ruka, a vengeful police officer in *Tokyo Gore Police* and Rikka, the cannibalistic Queen of Zombies in *Helldriver*.

Eihi started her career as an artist and model, and this has been a love throughout her life. Eihi is the director of a project that promotes art with themes such as 'Colours' and 'Flowers', conveying delicate beauty throughout her art.

What was it like growing up in Fukuoka, the largest city in Kyūshū?

I was born in Fukuoka, but from ages two to eleven I lived in various cities in Japan, including Hiroshima, Yamaguchi, and Tottori. Partly because of that, I changed schools three times. From an early age, I realised that life has encounters and farewells and that everything has a beginning and an end.

I still remember all the memories and scenery in each city vividly. When I was five years old in Hiroshima, I was sitting on the backyard block wall looking at the yellow field of rapeseed flowers, the kindergarten church I went to in Yamaguchi, and the bewitching red and black crow snakes I saw along the stream. Then, in contrast, the snowy scenery of Tottori and the smell of dust on the sand dunes, the scenery of cherry blossoms and spring that I have loved since I was a child. Also, all the memories of what I was thinking as I stood there are still alive in my heart.

Ever since I was a child, I have loved being alone. Of course, I had friends, but I always found time to think about various things by myself, draw pictures, read picture books, write poetry, and imagine various things about myself. I loved spending time with myself and this still hasn't changed.

At what point did you decide that you wanted to pursue a creative career, and were your family and friends supportive of this?

When I was a kid, I never envisioned myself doing creative work in the future. I never wanted to be a model or an actress. I had no interest in being in front of people. However, I had a hunch that someday I might be involved in a job that creates words and works, such as a writer, not as the subject matter. I believe that fate is a very mysterious thing.

On the other hand, when I was young, my mother thought that I would eventually become an artist. A best friend of mine since I was 15 says she felt like I would be in a creative career. The people around me probably knew me better than I knew myself. My family and friends are irreplaceable to me. The reason I can live like this is because they have changed, watched over me and supported me.

How did you get hired by Benetton as one of their models? And what was it like becoming so popular and well-known so quickly?

I was scouted during the summer vacation of my third year of high school, and the president of the agency that scouted me at the time took a snapshot of me. I was chosen and, before I knew it, I had to go to Paris to shoot as soon as I finished my high school graduation ceremony.

I didn't realise that I was going to be a model, and everything happened too quickly. Of course, this was my first trip abroad and my debut as a model. The shooting took a week. All foreign staff, including art director Oliviero Toscani, were confined to the studio, where the common languages were English and Italian. Other than me and another Japanese male model, all the other models were of various ethnicities from all over the world. I still remember that time vividly, the way to the studio, the time of the shooting, what I thought at that time, what I was doing, and the atmosphere of the makeup room. I didn't understand the details of English, but I was able to get a feel for the atmosphere, not the words. When I stood in front of the camera, I felt like I could naturally understand what I should do. I wasn't nervous at all. It

Tokyo Gore Police (2008)

was an exciting experience that can be expressed through sensations rather than words. The experience of creating work while spending time together with people of various races and from various places transcended national borders.

At the same time as thinking that it was a luxurious and valuable experience, I once again felt the vastness of the world. It was my first time shooting, but I was able to experience the fundamental meaning of creativity by going to Paris.

I consider my experience in Paris to be my starting point as an artist. When the filming was over and I returned to Japan, it was the university entrance ceremony. Originally, I didn't set out to become a model, so I really didn't think that I would continue after returning from Paris. However, somehow, I had a feeling that my future destiny would change because of all this.

After the shoot, I walked around Paris as much as possible until I returned to Japan. The Louvre, the Orsay Museum, the Palace of Versailles, the Eiffel Tower, the Seine River cruise, and Notre Dame Cathedral, I wanted to see as much as possible. At the time, I thought that I might never be able to come to Paris again.

The statue of Nike of Samothrace in the Louvre Museum is still my favourite sculpture. Its appearance is dynamic, noble, and divine, but it never seems to push you away; it seems to have blood in its veins. I think perfect things are great, but I don't think they're beautiful. However, the statue of Nike is missing in some places, and the figure of him trying to spread his wings and fly away without repairing his wounded figure is beautiful and touches my heart. At that time, I once again thought that I should live like this. When I look at the Nike statue, I feel like I can come back to being myself.

I then returned from Paris and went on to college as planned. In the fall, Benetton's Paris world advertisement shoot was put up on a large scale, and I decided to start modelling in Japan.

After moving the base of my

activities to Tokyo, I quickly came into the limelight, attracting attention in magazines, collections and numerous advertisements.

At that time, there was an Asian model boom, and it may have been the perfect timing for me to hit the wave of that era. My activities as a model lasted only about four years, and I was featured in countless media during that time. When I went to Paris, I felt like all my destinies began to move.

What made you decide to want to start acting?

I don't know. In 1997, when I was at the peak of my career as an international model, I suddenly decided to take a break. Cut off my long hair, which was a trademark at the time. The reason is that I wanted to reconsider my future. I wondered what would happen if I kept running like this, and before I knew it, I felt like I was standing in a terrible

place. People around me were against it, but I decided to stop and think again. In my hectic schedule, I was busy with my daily output.

The world of fashion is constantly changing. I took pride in my work as a model, and I still respect the designers and creators I worked with, but I wanted to do work where I could take my time and face challenges one by one.

The answer was the work of creating things as an artist, and the world of films. Art and films are things that remain unchanged and have never gone out of fashion for at least for 100 years. The more wonderful work is, the more it never goes out of existence. I think I wanted to create things in that world.

In your first film, Open House (1998), you played Mitsuwa. That is such a big role for any actor due to the depth of the character, showing the grim beauty in loneliness and pain. How did you get the role and how easy did you find the transition to acting?

This work is my debut as an actress, but at the time I was taking a break from modelling and creating works as an artist, while I was thinking about my future.

I had the opportunity to meet director Isao Yukisada, where we talked about many things as we created the role of Mitsuwa together. I had just turned down a role to appear in a TV drama series, but I thought that if I wanted to be an actress, I would be better off in a film.

At that time, Mr Yukisada, the producer, and my manager talked for about an hour at a cafe, but the content was not about the work, but rather casual and natural content.

The next time I was contacted, they asked me to play the lead role in this film. Then, this time, director Yukisada

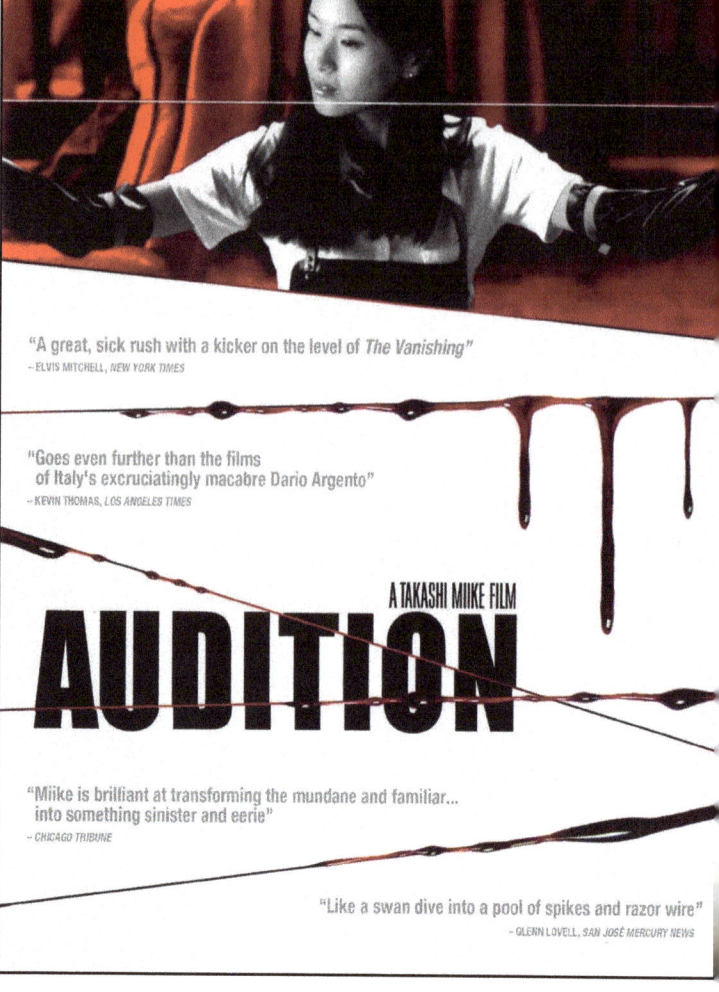

asked me to talk with him before filming started.

It was my first time acting as an actress, so I was a little nervous, but I trusted the director who said I could be myself and I was. I chose to live as Mitsuwa during the filming, leaning on Mitsuwa's loneliness.

The filming was done by a wonderful team of people who represent the Japanese film industry, the cameraman, Noboru Shinoda, and the lighting director, Yuki Nakamura, so every moment I was involved in was a gift and a wonderful experience. And above all, the talent of director Mr Yukisada was wonderful.

I really sympathised with his attitude and sensibility of carefully drawing a delicate psychological depiction. Even now, I still feel that I am glad that my debut film, as an actress, was this film and it was Mr Yukisada who directed it.

You released a book in the same year,

No Filter, Only Eyes, showcasing your photography and poems.

This book was featured at my photo exhibition in an art museum in Fukuoka. The main exhibition was a solo exhibition of photographic works and poetry works. Video works produced by myself were also presented at the venue. After taking a break from modelling, I studied photography with Mr Naoki, a world-famous photographer with whom I have been in contact both professionally and privately since I was a model.

This exhibition is a symbol of the time when I started working as a poet. Many people visited the venue every day, and it was a happy experience to have the opportunity to hold a solo exhibition at an art museum in my hometown, Fukuoka.

When I held my solo exhibition, I not only created and produced the work, but also designed and set up the venue, proofread the photo book, and designed the entrance ticket. This is because I wanted the people visiting the venue to directly feel the world view of the work that I created. It was the first project I worked on after taking a break from modelling.

How did you meet Takashi Miike and get the lead role as Asami in *Audition*?

I had read the original book some time ago and had been a fan of Mr Miike's work.

When I heard that Miike would be making a film of *Audition*, based on the novel by Ryu Murakami, I thought it would definitely be a very interesting project.

At that time, I heard that the director wanted to meet me, and I was eager to meet him. When I met with the director I didn't talk about the content of the work I was auditioning for, but the philosophical content of what I think about love between a man and a woman. I just said what I thought and, before I knew it, hours had passed. It wasn't a question of whether I would participate in the film or not, but the

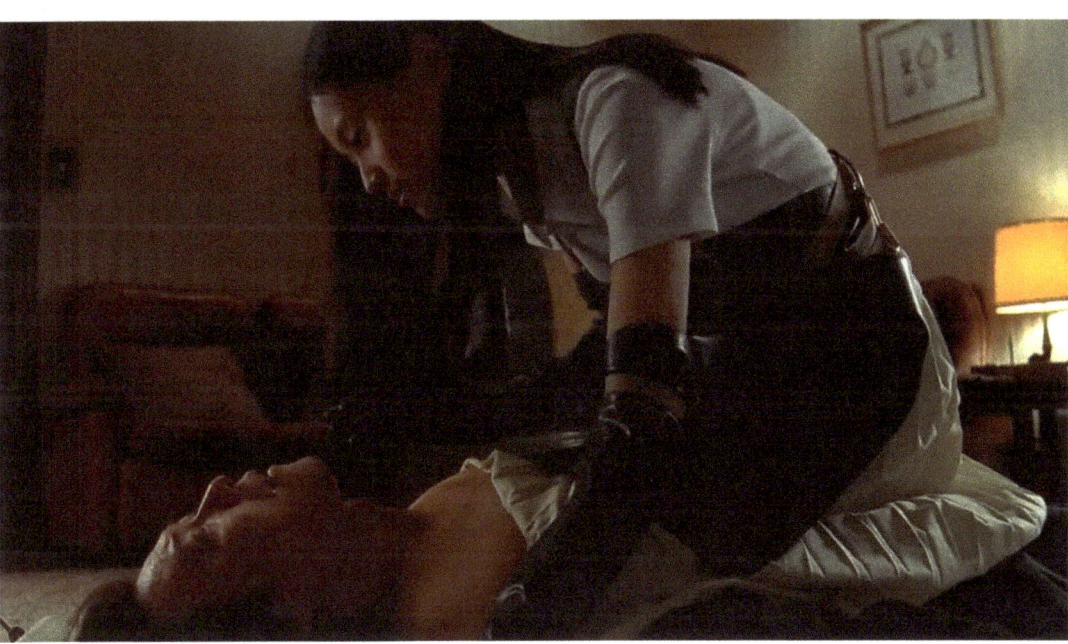

Audition (1999)

time spent simply talking with director Miike was a very good time for both of us.

Even though it was the first time we met, Mr Miike and I got into a lot of conversations, and the person running the event kept interrupting us by telling Mr Miike that we didn't have much time.

Finally, I told Mr Miike that I looked forward to watching the film *Audition* he was making, as it sounded interesting. I did not think I would be playing the role. The next day, Mr Miike contacted me and asked me to play Asami. I was surprised because I didn't think it would happen to me. It was a very strange and fateful moment.

Did you have any creative control over the character?

First of all, what I always try to do when acting, is to make myself feel

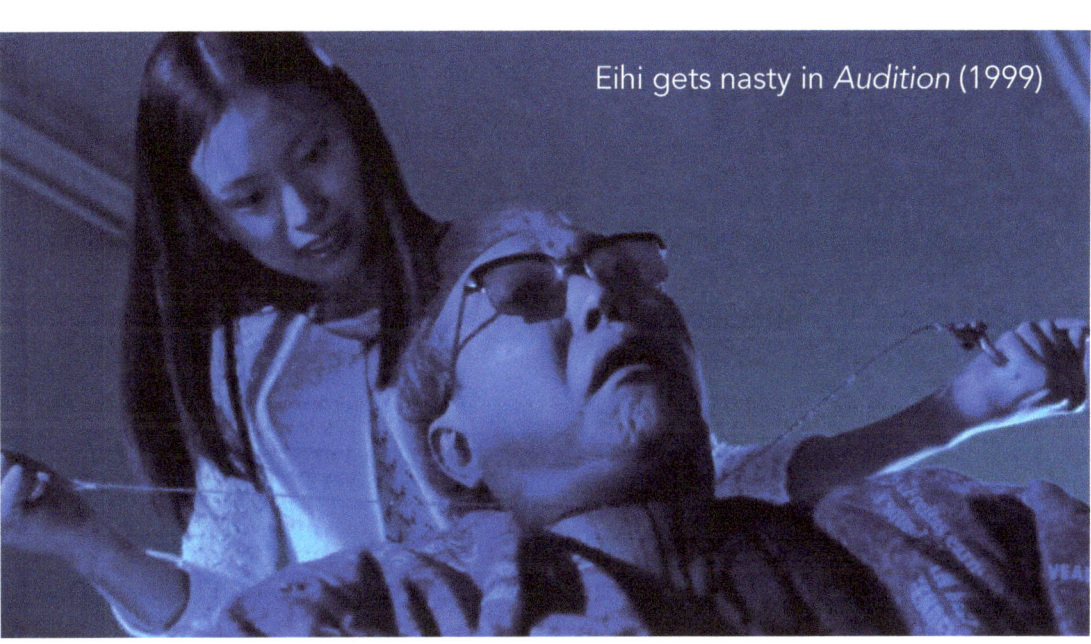

Eihi gets nasty in *Audition* (1999)

comfortable with the character I play.

For example, even if the character Asami is seen as a unique and difficult person to understand, by those around her, I, as the actor of Asami, must be the most understanding person, who stays close to her heart. Otherwise, I can't play the role, and I'm lying.

If I act while feeling uncomfortable with Asami, that lie will be reflected on the screen. In order for me to properly exist as Asami, I brought my heart close to her.

Upon reflection, how do you feel about Audition and what are your memories?

I don't think Audition is just a horror film. Asami is a sad person who cannot believe in the love of her partner. It may have been because of her impureness, but Aoyama always tried to be serious and faithful to Asami. But Asami couldn't accept that Aoyama had a world outside of hers. She ended up being what she was. She may have misrepresented her affection, but I think there is an unfulfilled hurtful sadness there.

Every day at the shooting site was a really creative and dense time. The script for that scene, the now-legendary "Kirikirikin" scene, was not originally in the script. On the day of the shoot, which I think was the last day of shooting, just before that scene, Mr Miike and I thought about the lines together. It was very natural for me. Maybe that's why the role of Asami naturally became closer to me.

Audition was released in 2023 in South Korea; the advertising and guests in attendance looked amazing. What can you tell us about it?

It was February 2023 when I got the news that Audition was officially screened in Korea - it was a contact from a Korean distribution company. Audition has been screened in countries around the world, such as the United States and Europe, but in South Korea, 23 years after the film was released, it became a reality.

A new Korean version of the film poster

has also been made, which is exciting. Public release was from April 19th, 2023. I am honoured that everyone involved in the Korean film industry and fans were looking forward to this screening.

You worked on several films and shorts after Audition, but it wasn't until you met Yoshihiro Nishimura that your career flourished again. How did you meet and what is he like as a person?

I met director Mr Nishimura in 2008 when I performed in Tokyo Gore Police and, since then, we have worked together on a variety of films.

In particular, Ruka from the Tokyo Gore Police is one of the most important characters to me, someone who cannot be replaced.

Mr Nishimura is a smart person, but his words, actions and beliefs change depending on the mood of the moment, so I feel that he is a person with a different set of values than mine.

I act based on universal philosophies and thoughts. I think he understands me as an actress, but on the other hand, I think he doesn't have much of a perspective or sense of values that captures my essence.

On the other hand, as a director, he has the instinct and talent to instantly come up with a clear answer and solve any tough situation during filming. He doesn't waste time or hesitate and has a positive attitude and judgment to resolve any incidents or troubles that occur on set. He is a very particular person, and I know that he trusts me to let me act freely.

I also think it is the actress's duty to respond to the director's feelings in my work.

I don't know if I will work with him again in the future, but at least not at the moment.

Eihi made a big international splash playing the unbalanced Asami in *Audition*

The first film you worked on was Tokyo Gore Police, which is insane! What did you think when you first heard of the concept and read the script?

My impression when I read the script was that there were a lot of cruel depictions; I wondered how it would turn out when it was made into a film. It was Nishimura's first directorial work, so it was difficult for me to imagine what it would be like. Now, I understand the atmosphere and composition of Mr Nishimura's works, but at the time I didn't have any of his works or samples to refer to. Mr Nishimura had already seen *Audition* at the time, and he had an image of me, but I didn't know anything about him. So, first of all, I thought I had to talk directly to him about who he was and how he was going to visualise his script. He thought that if I just understood the image in the director's mind, I would know what to do with this film. In order to build the role and image of the character Ruka and embody it in the film, I thought I should talk to the director first. As a result of talking, I was able to understand everything. At the time, Mr. Nishimura was shy and not very good at explaining things in words, but from the images he gave I was able to perfectly construct what I needed to do to play the role.

After that, I went into shooting thinking how much I could embody that image. It was a really tough shoot, and I had to risk my life to survive, but I did everything I could, so I have no regrets.

If I were asked to do the same shoot again now, I would definitely refuse because he is too hard in many ways.

You have worked a lot with Yoshihiro Nishimura, including Vampire Girl Vs. Frankenstein Girl (2008), Helldriver (2010), The Hell Chef segment from The Profane Exhibit (2013), The Ninja War of Torakage (2014) and Meatball Machine Kodoku (2017). Which were your favourites?

Each film has a place in my heart, but if I had to name one, it would be *Tokyo Gore Police*. From crank-in to crank-up,

there was no rehearsal, and 200 shots were taken in one day. It was a difficult time, but I think that it was because I was able to overcome that hardship with the director, that I was able to build a trusting relationship with him later on.

If I had to name another work, it would be The Ninja War of Torakage. I have participated in a number of director Nishimura's works so far, but the character I played in Torakage, Gensai Shinonome, is the last character that I really stood out for him in. After The Ninja War of Torakage, I have appeared in others but, for me, the work The Ninja War of Torakage is, in a sense, my own. I think that this role marked the end for me in that scene.

Having worked with many directors and actors, who have been your favourite people to work with?

Thankfully, all the directors I've met as an actor have been wonderful. Director Yukisada, who worked with me on my debut film, director Miike, director Shinji Aoyama, plus director Ryuhei Kitamura and director Takeshi Kitano, all of whom are talented people with different characters.

In particular, director Ryuhei Kitamura, even after so many years, still works on his creations with the unchanging purity and passion of a young boy. I would be happy if I could work with him again someday. There are many other stories I want to say, but there will not be enough pages to talk about them all.

Speaking of favourite actors, it's Koji Yakusho; I co-starred in Shinji Aoyama's Eureka and, after that, I had the opportunity to talk with him privately after the event. I believe that his acting ability is absolutely world-class. He's a great actor who can play normal people and can play crazy people perfectly. His usual appearance is very pure and eccentric. But he is also very simple and intuitive at heart. I want him to continue acting until he dies. He is the actor I admire the most.

Would you, or are there any plans, for sequels to any of your films, such as Audition or Tokyo Gore Police?

Thankfully, I always receive requests from people all over the world to make a sequel to Audition with my character. Before I retire from acting, it would be nice if I could do Audition 2. I don't know when I'll quit acting, so I'd like to do it now while I can.

What type of films or roles would you like to play in the future?

The role I would like to play is something like Willy Wonka with Johnny Depp in Tim Burton's Charlie and the Chocolate Factory. I've always loved this work, and I like the world of dark fantasy. Also, the character Willy Wonka is very close to me, and I think we are similar in many ways. I also like *The Addams Family*, so if I were to play the role, I think the role of Morticia would be perfect.

The UK had issues with film censorship until the late 1990s when we were able to see J-Horror and gore films. These genres now have a massive fan base.

How does it make you feel to know that you and your films are so well-known in popular culture here?

I am very honoured. I am very happy that people from all over the world have loved the works and characters that I have appeared in for such a long time. I believe that films are one of the forms of artistic expression, but it is the ideal form of art that the work continues to live on and be renewed in everyone's minds even many years after they have passed.

From the films you are famed for, you have a reputation as an intimidating, strong woman, not to be messed with (if you want to live!) How do you portray these characters so well? Is there a little bit of Asami inside you?

I am very honoured that the image of the film and the character I played has been appreciated. As for what kind of person I am, I think there are times when I can be close to the role, and times when I am not. Ultimately, I believe that the profession of an actor is only a medium and a role to express the work of the artist.

It is not important whether the character I play resembles the real me, but to realise the ideals that the director seeks, and to pursue expressions that reach the hearts of those who see the work in the end. What I can do is important to me. Just like Asami did during her audition, it's all about getting close to the role and sublimating and embodying what I feel, in a unique way, that only I can express. The closest thing might be to say that all the characters are me and not me.

You are concentrating now on your first passion; art, photography and poetry. Can you please tell us about this?

For several years until 2021, I had a lot of things to think about, so I took a break from activities. And since I restarted my activities in 2021, as an artist, it has become my main passion. You can see what

Eihi plays a mother possessed by a demon starfish in *Helldriver* (2010)

Eihi cameos in Meatball Machine Kodoku

kind of work I do on my official website and Instagram; *https://www.instagram.com/eihi.shiina_official*.

I am also working on a trilogy of films that I direct, write and star in. In addition, last year, we launched a web museum called 'Eihi Shiina Kotonoha Photo Project', which presents my works as an artist. We sell worldwide (*https://eihi.secret.jp/*)

Models and actors are jobs that are used as objects in another person's work. After working in that industry for many years, the answer I arrived at was to go back to my roots and create ideas from scratch, just as I did in 1999.

I am working on my own comprehensive art that integrates all of the knowledge and creative thoughts I have acquired along the way. There is more than one way of self-expression, and that's when I realised I was the only one who could master all of these expressions myself as an actress, a model, a writer and as a photographer. However, everything is based on the concept of words ('Kotonoha'), and I intend to include words that resonate across various languages and borders in my work. I would like to deliver the comprehensive art of Eihi Shiina, which I am working on, to everyone, one by one.

With your photography, I like your use of space and the contrasts of your vivid colours.

Unlike video, photographic expression is an expression that captures a moment and makes it last forever. It is a delicate world in which the meaning changes depending on the balance of colours, light and shadow, the way you stand, the way you look, the angle of your neck, and the wind blowing in your hair.

As a subject and as a photographer who captures it, I create a worldview by thinking about the meaning of each theme and the situation from both sides. I direct all processes, including costumes and hair and makeup.

All of the works in which I myself am the subject are self-portraits. I believe

that photography is not just a form of expression, it is simply beautiful. Joy, sorrow, anger, hesitation, wishes... in order to confront the various words ('Kotonoha') of the heart, and express their existence in photographs, it is necessary to know the shape of one's own mind and body.

There are times when the power of existence is released to the maximum, and depending on the situation, there are worlds that are beautifully established by erasing the presence of things, just like an object.

There is not one answer, and the correct answer is different every time depending on the theme. Photographs of the sky, photographs of flowers, and whether or not I am the subject, I capture the moment that exists before my eyes and work with the feeling of sublimating it into an everlasting art form.

The minimalism in your art also shows the quiet beauty of your subject matter.

First of all, I look at the existence of the subject, and that person is the most beautiful, and I create a situation where the existence could bloom in its own way. My approach to art is to capture and express the moment, unwavering and eternal.

Your art is very popular, being sold on your website. You're now taking pre-orders on your new material. Where do you envision your art career going?

I am very happy and honoured that the words I have put into my art have been perceived and accepted as messages that transcend language barriers and various national borders. There is something I always think about and wish for. It is my wish that art should not be something that is far from my daily life, but something that

is close to people's lives and hearts. The reason why I created a museum shop on my website is because I want everyone to enjoy my art. The Mona Lisa in the Louvre cannot be displayed at home, but if you order my art, you can enjoy it every day.

All items are created one by one after receiving an order and delivered with a handwritten message and signature. I would appreciate it if you could feel the light by having my work by your side when you are sad, happy, cheerful or not.

From now on, I will continue to create new works, and I would like to deliver art that is close to everyone's life and heart. And someday, I would like to hold exhibitions where people can come into contact with my art, not only in Japan, but also in various continents such as Europe, America, and Asia.

As an actress, I have been invited to film festivals around the world, but it would be wonderful if I could travel to various countries with my art as an artist, Eihi Shiina.

What are your plans for the future and is there anything else you are currently working on?

Currently I'm focusing on my art projects and I'm also working on a film trilogy that I directed, wrote, and starred in. Having said that, at the moment we don't have a sponsor, and we're doing everything independently, so we're having a hard time because it's not as speedy as normal film production. So I want to complete this trilogy first, and when it is completed, I would like everyone in the world to see it.

I would like to be invited to film festivals and, above all, I hope that I will be able to reunite with people all over the world and meet new people through this work.
This is the culmination of my journey

Eihi starts to mutate in *Tokyo Gore Police* (2008)

and the art I have been working on.

As an actress, I am still receiving requests to appear in films and, in 2023, I will be appearing in several new films. In addition, I plan to respond to various offers on a global scale, including artist activities.

Do you have any last words for us?

Thank you for the questions. What I talked about in this interview is all of my thoughts on film, art and the artwork. As an actress and an artist, I look forward to meeting more people around the world.

Thank you very much for speaking with us and we wish you all the best for the future.

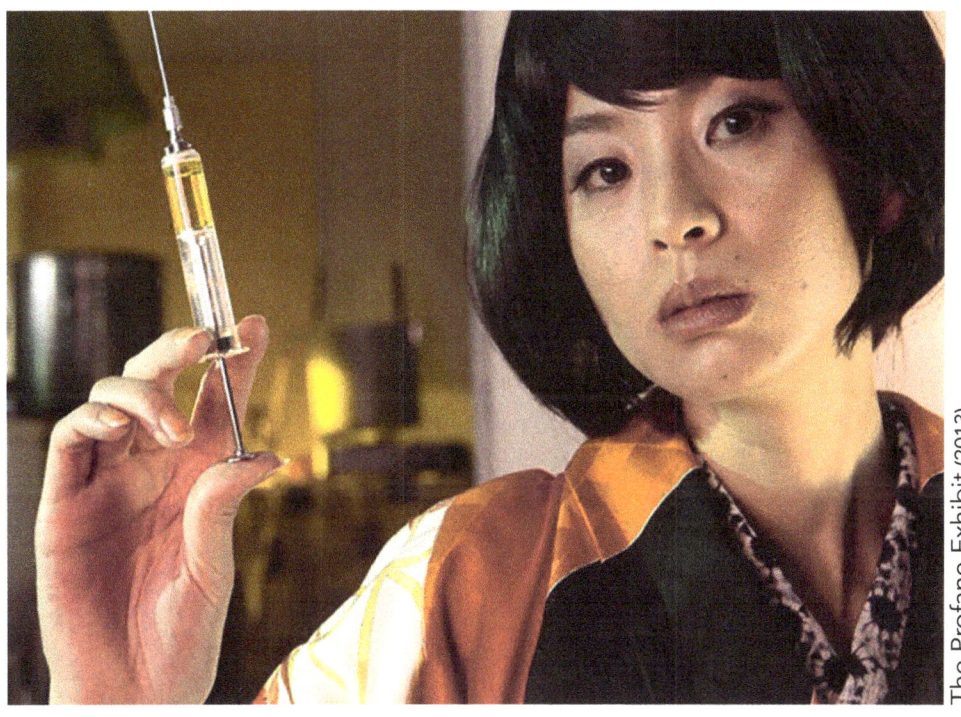

The Profane Exhibit (2013)

HOPPING MADNESS!

By Hamma Horra

A look at hopping vampires in a post-Lam Ching-Ying world…

I'm sure many of us know, love and very probably own multiple copies, in various formats, of Ricky Lau's sublime 1985 smash hit *Mr Vampire*.

The film brought the jiangshi (aka hopping vampire) craze to a worldwide audience, establishing many of the genre's tropes and solidifying Lam Ching-Ying as the ultimate vampire-busting, yellow-robed Taoist master.

This classic birthed hundreds of homages and straight-up copycats, TV shows, video games, comics, board games and stationery sets. Pretty much anything you could think of could be found with a grinning jiangshi in Hong Kong, South Korea and Japan in the early nineties.

Even though Sammo Hung's *Hocus Pocus*, *Encounters of the Spooky Kind* and *The Dead and the Deadly* (all co-starring Lam Ching-Ying) - plus even Hammer's cult classic *Legend of the 7 Golden Vampires* had already established the kung fu horror crossover to great success, it was this enjoyable Golden Harvest fantasy horror hit, produced by Sammo Hung, that blew up the genre.

The great Lam Ching-Ying starred in 4 of the 5 official films, the spin-off TV show and also starred in or at least cameoed as the stoic, one-browed

daoshi (Taoist priest) in dozens of other jiangshi/ghost films in the late 80s and early 90s.

The Ching-Ying directed *Vampire vs Vampire* (1989) introduced western vampires to the mix, *Magic Cop* (1990) set the spooky action in modern-day Hong Kong with Lam playing a Taoist cop battling Japanese black magic, whilst *The Ultimate Vampire* (1991) played out as a spin-off of *Mr Vampire*, including Chin Siu-Ho as the happy-go-lucky sidekick.

Crazy Safari (1991) was an unofficial sequel to the south African comedy film *The Gods Must Be Crazy* that saw the hero priest team-up with tribesman N!xau in a story that even boasts the ghost of Bruce Lee in a cameo!

The Wizard's Curse (1992) and *Skin Striperess* (1992) featured the famed daoshi in CAT III romps and *The Musical Vampire* (1992) was another *Mr Vampire* spin-off, this time with a jiangshi controlled by music.

A fanged fiend from *Spiritual Trinity* (2008)

Lam Ching-Ying's vampire expert also pops up in *An Eternal Combat*, *Red and Black*, *Spiritual Trinity* and *Midnight Conjure* - all from 1991.

In 1992 came *Mad Mad Ghost*, *Forced Nightmare*, *Banana Spirit* and *Exorcist Master*, a film directed by Wu Ma, who also made *The Chinese Ghostbuster* in 1994.

While the hopping undead film craze was wreaking havoc on Hong Kong cinemas, the rest of Asia was just as eager to get in on the action. Taiwan produced loads of jiangshi films, possibly beating Hong

Lam Ching-Ying was the Van Helsing of Asian vampire movies

Page 15 Film Frenzy

Kong's output, including the already mentioned *Exorcist Master*. Taiwan also popularised the sub-genre of child jiangshi with the *Hello Dracula* movie series that was cut up into half-hour instalments and aired on Japanese TV as the mini series *Yugen Doushi 2*. Taiwan was also responsible for *Aloha, The Little Vampire* (featuring Charng Shan), *New Mr Vampire 2*, and *Spirit vs Zombi* (1988).

South Korea gave us the bonkers *The Aliens and Hong Kong Zombie* (1989), where a flying saucer shoots strange rays over a cemetery, awakening a group of vampire children who end up in a conflict with gangsters. Korea was also responsible for *Gang-Si Training Center*, and *The Smart Little Kang-si*, both from 1988.

Malaysia was behind 2015's bizarre vanity project, for snack shop owner Jaguar Lim, called *The Zombies vs The Lucky Exorcist*.

And we might not ever get to see the footage filmed for the cancelled *Demon Hunters*, a western audience

remake of *Mr Vampire*, starring Yuen Wah, Jack Scalia and the Mamas and Papas singer Michelle Phillips!

We did, however, get to see an English language take on the genre with the release of John Fasano's Canadian/Japanese production *The Jitters* (1989). The film's plot concerned Chinatown toughs murdering a local businessman, who returns as a revenge-focused jiangshi. The novelty of seeing Chinese hopping vampire folklore used in a low budget horror flick from an American director is made more enjoyable thanks to the appearance of the always reliable James Hong.

After watching Chinese vampires versus European vampires, vampire kids, jiangshi pornography in *Ghoul Sex Squad* (1991)

and even hopping vampires fighting a cheap knock-off of Robocop in Filmark International's strange, trashy, fun *Robo Vampire* (1988), audience members were starting to tire of the genre - and then, to cap it off, there was the tragic, untimely passing of Lam Ching-Ying during planning for the 3rd season of *Vampire Expert*, which led to hopping ghouls and their ying-yang clad arch nemesis priest having a short rest in their coffins.

But, much like their Transylvanian cousin, they weren't left ignored for long, because a whole generation of filmmakers, who grew up with the genre, were eager to bring back these iconic, supernatural denizens - and soon they started to create their own spins on the genre.

Over the years many attempts to restart or cash in on the success of *Mr Vampire* have emerged, with Juno Mak's visually stunning *Rigor Mortis* (2013) being the most successful. In

In recent years China has upped its production of jiangshi films. In *The Legend Returns* (2020) and *Taoist Priest* (2021) the actors Ge Shuai and Zhang Dicai don heavy makeup and fake eyebrows to mimic Lam Ching-Ying's iconic character look. But these later examples play out like low budget mainland TV fare with a lot of the creativity & great choreography from the 80s and 90s heyday sadly missing.

Hopping vampires won't be away from the cinema screen and TV anytime soon, though, that's for sure. Even the South Korean director of *Train to Busan* (2016), Yeon

The Legend Returns (2020)

Sang-ho, has stated in interviews that he intends to make a jiangshi film.

Fans of these flicks are waiting patiently for that one future classic hopping vampire film to truly bring back the spotlight on the much-loved horror genre.

Hopefully, filmmakers will stop the impossible task of replacing or mimicking the awesome Lam Ching-Ying and will focus instead on creating a new and exciting path that carries on the traditions presented in *Mr Vampire*, which will bring smiles to the faces of Taoism vs undead fans worldwide.

it, original *Mr Vampire* cast members Chin Siu-Ho, Billy Lau and the excellent Chung Fat (continuing the 'if you can't get Lam Ching-Ying, get Chung Fat' trend) experience eerie goings-on in a run-down apartment building.

Other examples of the genre's return are *Vampire Controller* (2001), *Vampire Super* (2007) and *Vampire Warriors* (2010), all with Yuen Wah, then there's *Sifu vs Vampire* (2014), *Vampire Clean-up Department* (2017) and *Mr Zombie* (2018), which stars Chin Siu-Ho.

Taoist Priest (2021)

GRACE AND GRIT

MOON LEE

Interviewed by Justyn Hughes

Moon Lee Choi-Fung, born on 14th February 1965, is a renowned former actress and stuntwoman from Hong Kong, celebrated for her roles in the action and martial arts film and TV sectors. She's recognized especially for her contributions to the 'girls with guns' sub-genre.

Between the ages of 6 and 12, Lee lived in Kaohsiung, Taiwan, due to her father's business endeavours. During this time, she honed her Mandarin Chinese language skills and pursued her interests in piano and dance, resulting in numerous performances.

Upon her return to Hong Kong for middle school, Lee faced challenges with her Cantonese fluency, which was somewhat unpolished. At 15, her talents were recognised by television director Siu Hin-fai, during a school dance recital. This led to her role as A Mun in the TV series *Fatherland*. This character resonated with her so deeply that many affectionately began addressing her as A Mun. Her remarkable portrayal paved the path into the world of acting, and her dance background served as a foundation for executing intricate action sequences.

After high school, at the age of 18, Lee secured contracts with Asia Television and Golden Harvest. During a promotional trip to Japan with Mitsubishi, she adopted the English moniker 'Moon', inspired by the Cantonese pronunciation of 'Mun'.

Moon Lee's acting journey includes over 400 TV episodes, then a pivot into primarily action films.

As the 1990s concluded, she moved away from the film industry, channeling her passion into promoting dance. She founded a dance school, nurturing the next generation of dancers, many of whom have garnered accolades in Hong Kong dance contests.

As a testament to her commitment, Lee endured a harrowing accident while filming a stunt for *Devil Hunters* in 1989. A mistimed explosion led to third-degree burns on her face and hands. This incident, and a tribute to her tenacity, is documented in the film's epilogue.

Moon Lee is simply one of the greatest female fighters in Hong Kong martial arts film history. Her high tempo fight scenes and hard-hitting action ranks her up among the greats, along with Angela Mao, Cynthia Rothrock and Yukari Oshima.

Some of her early movie roles which spring to mind are as follows... *Zu: Warriors From The Magic Mountain*, *The Champions*, *Those Merry Souls*, and *The Protector*. After that we got to see her in the first two of the classic *Mr Vampire* films, but it wasn't until *Angel (Iron Angels)* was released that we finally got to see what she could really do. The 'Girls with Guns' genre was born! Moon teamed up with Yukari Oshima and delivered big time, showing that females could fight as well and act as tough as men do and, wow, she was not wrong! Moon then starred in such films as *Devil Hunters* (1989), *Fatal Termination* (1990), *The Nocturnal Demon* (1990), where she treated viewers to some awesome roller skate kung fu, and *Beauty Investigator* (1992). Then, as mentioned, she stepped away from making movies in around 1995, to focus on dancing - something she did way before becoming a film star - but she did make a return in 2008 for the film *Only The Way*, a low budget movie about a man whose life is transformed by Buddhist teachings.

Here Moon Lee talks about some of her movies, working with favourite actors and also the injuries sustained on set. I want to personally thank Moon for taking time and doing this interview...

Early in your career you starred with legends such as Yuen Biao and Sammo Hung, in movies like *Zu Warriors*, *The Champions* and *Winners And Sinners*. How did working with them first come about?

I was introduced to Yuen and Sammo when I signed a contract with Golden Harvest. They were all supportive of me and said I had a future doing more action movies. But I am not a martial artist per se, so they gave me several people who could teach me kung fu. It was easy to learn because I already knew ballet. So all I needed to do was integrate kung fu moves into my knowledge of ballet and dance steps.

You have done some incredible action, fights and stunts in your movies, which is why you're such a favourite amongst action movie fans. What are the worst injuries you sustained whilst filming?

Injuries while shooting *Devil Hunters*. I sustained heavy burns and was in hospital recovering for days... I think that was the worst, aside from a broken wrist, ankles, and a dislocated thumb.

Mr Vampire II (1986)

You worked with a favourite Hong Kong actor of mine, Lam Ching-Ying, early in your career. What was it like starring with him and did you learn from him when filming on set?

Lam Ching-Ying was a great actor, a legend and a friend.

I respected him a lot. He gave me pointers on discipline and helped me on proper choreography.

He taught me many things, not just in film making, but about life as well.

If you could introduce someone famous to your films, to star alongside, who would you pick and why?

I would introduce Ms Nora Miao to play someone in my films.

I have utmost respect for her. She would not have to do action scenes with me, but just to have her there would be an honour.

What do you make of the current martial arts movie actors - and do you think the glory days of Golden Harvest and Shaw Brothers will ever be topped?

Today... the action, I think, has already shifted from Hong Kong to Hollywood, which is good for the actors because they are working in a safe environment compared to our era. But I do not think it will top Golden Harvest or Shaw Brothers.... I do not see that ever happening.

How would you like to be remembered in years to come for your movie career?

I would love to be remembered, especially if it helps aspiring young actors to understand that you need to be dedicated, disciplined and hard working in order to be successful.

The uniqueness of my era needs to be remembered too, the fact that I achieved success in an industry that had been really male dominated.

Finally, what would you like to say to your fans around the world and to the readers?

Hello, this is Moon Lee.

I just want to thank my followers for your continued support, keeping my legacy alive and well - hopefully for generations to come. I wouldn't be as I am now without your continued patronage for my films.

Fēi cháng gàn xiè! •

Angel 2 (1988)

BRETT RATNER PUBLISHES THE NEW ESSENTIAL GUIDE TO HONG KONG MOVIES...

...AND SUPERSTAR JACKIE CHAN WRITES THE BOOK'S FOREWORD!

To mark the upcoming release of THE NEW ESSENTIAL GUIDE TO HONG KONG MOVIES Hollywood director *Brett Ratner* remembers when he first met Jackie Chan and explains why he decided to publish the new version of the much-loved Essential Guide...

When Rick Baker reached out to me to say that he was working on re-launching *Eastern Heroes Magazine*, and intended to put me on the cover with Jackie Chan and Chris Tucker, I was hesitant at first to accept the invitation because we hadn't done a *Rush Hour* film in over fifteen years, but Rick's persistence, perseverance and passion for the *Rush Hour* films got me to relent.

When I received a copy of the magazine and read Rick's interview with me, I was surprised by the overwhelming flood of emotions and memories I experienced as I remembered my time spent with Jackie Chan and Chris Tucker making the three *Rush Hour* movies.

Brett still refers to Jackie as his 'Big Brother'

These *Rush Hour* films completely changed the course of my life, but it wasn't the giant box office or success that changed me, it was the twenty five year friendship with Jackie - a legendary actor who I still refer to as Big Brother. Jackie utterly altered my life the minute he agreed to star in *Rush Hour*.

As someone who had spent hundreds of hours watching Shaw Brothers and Golden Harvest films during my youth, making home movies filled with kung fu, hip hop and nunchakus, emulating my heroes Jackie Chan and Bruce Lee, I never imagined that I would not only meet Jackie Chan, but would also direct him in three blockbuster films!

When I flew to Johannesburg (because Jackie was in South Africa filming *Who Am I?*) to pitch the first *Rush Hour* script, I explained to Jackie that I knew why the American-made films *The Cannonball Run*, *The Big Brawl* and *The Protector* hadn't worked in the United States and had alienated his core Asian audience. I told him I knew how to make a film that would deliver to the US audience and keep his Asian fans satisfied too. I admitted that I could never deliver action that would compare to his *Police Story* series or *Project A*. I said that what I wanted to do was make a true hybrid of Hong Kong and Hollywood filmmaking: I would focus on the characters but leave the action up to him. It was very bold of me to say that I personally loved watching a 20-minute Jackie Chan fight sequence, but that it would not fly with US audiences. I suggested that we would have to take the same 20-minute fight and cut it down to the best two minutes. As I saw it, US audiences were going to the movies to fall in love with the characters and the story, while Hong Kong audiences were primarily satisfied with great action. I also told him that in most of his movies, his stunt men played the roles of villains. American audiences want to hate the villain as much as they loved the hero, so I wanted to surround him with top actors within the atmosphere of a thriller, but keep his physical comedy throughout, along with Chris Tucker's verbal comedy. Ultimately, it would be a fish out of water comedy in the tone of a thriller.

Jackie was impressed with my knowledge of Hong Kong cinema, but I started to feel my pitch wasn't convincing him. He had made movies for longer than I had been alive at that point. I think he was mostly struck by my sincerity when I handed him the script and told him that, though I loved the idea of the movie, this particular draft sucked, but I was going to hire a talented young writer named Jeff Nathanson to rewrite it. I left lunch without a clue about what Jackie's response would be. At least I was going to be able to tell my future grandchildren about the time I flew to South Africa just to have lunch with Jackie Chan. A week later, my agent called and gave me the news: Jackie Chan was going to do *Rush Hour*!

The dream finally became a reality when I introduced Jackie to Chris Tucker. Chris expressed his enthusiasm for Jackie and admiration for his work, and Jackie graciously articulated his excitement about us working together. After the meeting, Chris asked me to walk with him outside for a private conversation. As soon as we stepped out of the door, he said in his high-pitched tone, "I really like Jackie Chan, Bratt (he still calls me Bratt, by the way), but he doesn't speak a word of English! How are we going to make a movie if he doesn't speak any English?" I reassured Chris that everything would be fine and when I went back in and asked Jackie what he thought about Chris, he said, "I really like him, but I don't understand anything he's saying!" I knew right then and there that they were going to be brilliant together. They literally didn't understand a word they were saying to each other, but they had a chemistry that was out of my control. So, when Jackie was stuck with his English in a scene, I would signal Chris to say "Do you understand the words coming out of my mouth?" That was real! Jackie really didn't understand the words coming out of Chris's mouth. And that is why the fish out of water comedy worked in these movies. In the first *Rush Hour* film Jackie's character Lee came from Hong Kong to LA and didn't speak the language, in *Rush Hour 2* Chris's character Carter came to Hong Kong and was the fish out of water, and in *Rush Hour 3* they both went to Paris and both couldn't speak the language.

With their language barrier and their fondness for each other, I knew that when I turned the cameras on, the element that is so vital to making a

Jackie receives his honorary Oscar!

successful buddy action picture would flood the screen: CHEMISTRY. To this day, I believe that Jackie and Chris still don't understand the words coming out of each other's mouths, but what they do understand is what makes a great on-screen duo.

Rush Hour was an amalgamation of Hong Kong action, buddy cop films, fish out of water comedy, with a great villain and a brilliant Lalo Schifrin score. To me, Lalo was as important as the main actors. I wanted to work with him long before I ever became a director. My favourite score is from the Bruce Lee classic film Enter the Dragon, which was a big inspiration because it mixed funky urban grooves with Chinese instrumentations. Lalo created a score for Rush Hour that had elements of his 70s coolness with an updated, hard-edged action tone. It's evocative and propelling, threatening and thrilling - all at once. Lalo's music is a character unto its own.

During the shooting of the first Rush Hour film, once I started feeling comfortable with Jackie, revelling in the glory of sitting next to him on set, I asked the question that I had been contemplating since the day I was told he would do the film; "Jackie, why did you do this film with me?" He looked me straight in the eye and explained that lots of big producers and directors had come to Hong Kong over the years to convince him to be in their films because they had the best scripts in Hollywood. Jackie said that he'd translate the scripts and would realise within the first ten pages how bad the stories were. Jackie said to me that I was the first filmmaker ever to tell the truth when I said that my script sucked but I knew what was needed to make it work. He went on to say I was honest with him like a kid, so he decided to take a shot with me, and he was happy he did because he believed it was worth the chance, in spite of all his bad experiences in Hollywood!

Thank you, Jackie, for your generous spirit and believing in a scrappy young director whose dreams you made come true.

After the Eastern Heroes Magazine article triggered all these memories, I continued to talk with Rick, who introduced me to Ken Miller, who I had many great conversations with about some of the Hong Kong movies we all grew up loving, from Five Fingers of Death to Drunken Master.
I couldn't get enough of the Hong Kong movie talk and immediately suggested my interest in publishing a new, updated version of The Essential Guide to Hong Kong Movies.

God bless Rick and Ken for producing this new edition and sharing their love for the golden age of Hong Kong cinema with the rest of us!

COMING OUT IN 2024!

Extensively revised and expanded, including over 670 film reviews, a poster gallery, a look at the key studios that made Hong Kong cinema so amazing, a foreword by internatinal action-king Jackie Chan & afterwords from the awesome Cynthia Rothrock and the equally dynamic Vincent Lyn!

Published by RatPac Press and Skyhorse Publishing
Distributed by Simon & Schuster

FILM FRENZY REVIEWS

ASIAN HORROR, FANTASY, SCIENCE FICTION AND CULT MOVIES

MUTANT GHOST WARGIRL (2022)

Starring Mu Qimiya, Li Mingxuan, Liu Beige, Cui Zhenzhen, Zheng Yan, Shang Na, Deng Haowen
Written by Xiao Ye
Directed by Liu Binjie
Produced by Xu Hao, Du Jian, Wang Rui
Cappu films/Error 404 Productions

In 2077, at a time when gene tech has advanced immeasurably, private consortiums invest in gene mutation research, developing warriors with super abilities for use in underground death-combat competitions. In order to keep on top of the increasing mutant crime, the International Security Alliance Organization has been established.

Ghost (Qimiya) is an ISAO operative who has been captured by the crime group Medusa Consortium in Korea. Ghost had been on an undercover mission, using the name Wu, but the Medusa Consortium has experimented on her, injecting her with genetic induction solution, resulting in Ghost acquiring powers and losing her memory, so when smart-suited members of the International Security Alliance Organization storm into an experimentation chamber to save her, Ghost/Wu doesn't know what the hell is happening to her. A shoot-out ensues and it seems that the ISAO operatives are owning the situation... until a huge, slavering mutant monster is unleashed on them! This beast has a maw full of pink, squid-like tentacles and can split open its face like the Demogorgon from *Stranger Things*. Ghost kicks into action and slices off some of the creature's tentacle-tongues, but, as she attempts to escape, a slinky, leather-clad female Medusa agent with a sharp, blonde wig and super abilities, including teleportation and telekinesis powers, gets in her way, forcing Ghost to unleash her own still-developing mutation-induced skills to do battle with blondie.

Ghost finally breaks out of the chamber (hidden at the back of a plastic surgery hospital), blacks out and wakes up in an apartment, owned by nice-guy special agent Zhou Yang (Mingxuan). As the plot progresses, we're introduced to various villains and learn of the different categories of super-humans that have been artificially created, including Class A, Class B and S-Class mutants.

Ghost, who can move so fast that time seems to stand still, also has enhanced strength and is very handy with a long blade. Her powers seem to vary and are not clearly defined, and she uses some skills more sparingly than others.

Opponents she faces-off against include Class A mutant Cui Youxi, who can encase her arm in rocks and can manipulate stone & cement weapons, S-Class mutant Angela,

German DVD cover

who has healing powers, plus high-ranking Medusa baddie Li Yongshun, who boasts heightened telekinesis as one of his gifts.

Though we are led to believe that we'll be witnessing some illegally-streamed, gladiatorial-style death matches, we see very little of them. That's not to say that we don't get mutant-powered fights, which are mainly showdowns that occur between ghost and her various pursuers. The skirmish between Angela and Ghost is resolved quicker than expected, especially considering Angela is meant to be a really tough S-Class mutant, but the end fight confrontation focusing on a blade-wielding Ghost going up against Yongshun is better, with Ghost seemingly outclassed at first, getting telekinetically hurled around an opulent room, smashing into walls and pillars, spitting out gouts of blood as she's injured. Even when she starts fighting back she has to contend with her opponent filling the air with hundreds of glass shards.

Ultimately, *Mutant Ghost Wargirl* doesn't live up to the promise of its beginning, where we were treated to shots of Ghost and the ISAO agents fighting the massive muto-monster and the sexy, bewigged blonde Medusa agent in the experimental chamber. Nothing that follows manages to be quite as good or as outlandish as that opening sequence.

But the film, which is quite obviously influenced by *Akira* (hologram-festooned future cityscapes & some similar-sounding choral music), *Ghost in the Shell* (geisha robots) and *X-Men* (super-powered mutants), does manage to always look good. There are some fun, high-kicking battling babe scraps, some decent quality, detailed CGI effects, and the art direction is consistently eye-catching, meaning that this Chinese flick, though superficial and far from original, never outstays its welcome.

SNIPER: VENGEANCE (2023)

Starring Yu Rongguang, Xing En, Jane Wu, Nicholas Pierre Bruechert, Lizzan Latif, Yan Desheng
Written by Yang Zhe, Chang Xu, Liu Laisong
Directed by Vash

While on a mission somewhere in Southeast Asia, ace sniper Captain Gao (Rongguang) of Storm Squad survives a lethal ambush but is framed and accused of betraying his squad. Hunted by both his former colleagues and the villainous Ghost Team, Gao is captured by Storm Squad, but escapes from a plane mid-flight, parachuting down to the jungle island base of Ghost Team, which has kidnapped energy expert scientists to help create a sonic weapon of mass destruction.

Yu Rongguang is mature and solid as the lead character Gao in this action pic from Chinese streamer Youku, a film stuffed with loads of full-auto firefights, splattery blood squibs and characters who love to lob grenades, though the movie doesn't actually feature much in the way of sniping, apart from during the opening and at the end. This serviceable final act sees Gao perform a pretty far-fetched fan-assisted killshot, before he takes part in the destruction of a super-cannon, though this does entail (as so often happens in new Chinese movies) an act of self-sacrifice.

Sniper: Vengeance features science fiction-tinged story elements, such as a minigun that skitters around on robot legs as it fires rocket-propelled bullets, and the aforementioned infrasonic cannon, which we never really see put to devastating use, other than when it is test-fired to kill a large flock of birds.

All in all, *Sniper: Vengeance* is watchable and also forgettable in just about equal measure.

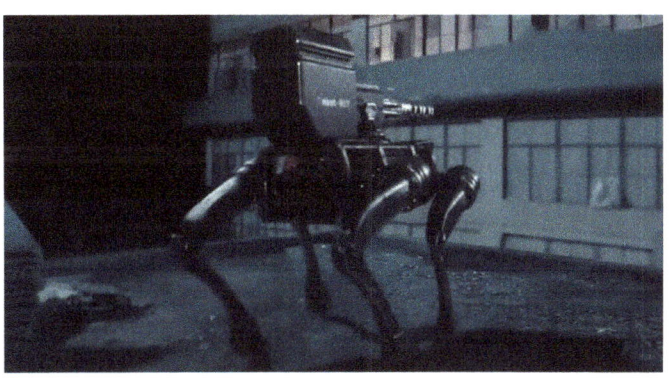

WARRIORS OF FUTURE (2022)

Starring Louis Koo, Lau Ching-Wan, Philip Keung, Carina Lau, Tse Kwan Ho, Wan Guopeng, Wu Qian, He Guoxuan, So Yuet-Yin
Written by Lau Ho-Leung, Mak Tin-Shu
Directed by Ng Yuen Fai
Produced by Tang Wai-But
One Cool Film Production/Media Asia Films/Hua Wen Movie Group

Various wars and the ongoing destruction of the environment lead to an increase in dangerous toxins in the air, so the people of a desperate future Earth begin to build Skynet domes in the hope of providing better air for its citizens, but a meteorite crashes earthwards, releasing a giant, ever-growing alien plant that begins to infest an urban region known as B16. This voracious vegetation, codenamed Pandora, expands in deadly bursts during rainfall, and a squad of soldiers from B16's Air Combat Unit are sent on a mission to locate Pandora's hidden pistil (its reproductive centre) so that they can detonate a 'gene bullet' that will hopefully reprogram the plant to become a docile cleanser of Earth's atmosphere… but our heroes must do this before the next major rainstorm, or the authorities will be forced to heavily bomb Pandora, which will result in a heavy loss of human life in the surrounding city. To make matters even more difficult, there is a traitor who wants this mission to fail…

The visuals for *Warriors of Future* can sometimes become really overloaded with CGI, but at least the quality of the special effects is much better than those seen in similar flicks. We get to see vast, vine-shrouded cityscapes, some tilt-rotor aircraft firing at angry plant appendages, collapsing buildings and crashing military hardware. The helmer of this Hong Kong action-sci-fi fest is Ng Yuen Fai, who usually works as a visual effects supervisor, so it's hardly surprising this production is chock-full of special effects eye candy.

After the attack fleet gets heavily depleted, partly due to sabotage, the few surviving soldiers are aided by military desk jockey Johnson Cheng (Ching-Wan) and an oddball ex-soldier called Skunk (Keung). With time running out, the group attempts to complete their mission, but now they must defend themselves from swarms of human-sized crustacean/bug creatures too! These alien critters have mandibles, teeth, four eyes, can communicate using their vibrating neck-plates, and resemble feral versions of the 'prawns' from *District 9* (2009). As I'm an avid movie monster fan, I was happy, of course, to see these beasties, though from a plot perspective they do tend to make

you forget that the Pandora plant, often dormant and offscreen between rainfall scenes, is supposed to be the main threat. It is eventually revealed, however, that these chitinous creatures actually originate from Pandora's pistil.

Characterisations are sketchy, with Tyler (Koo) given the kind of parent-grieving-a-dead-child backstory we've seen too many times before, whilst quirky Skunk is provided with a minor character arc when he proves himself to be a dependable soldier once more. Lau Ching-Wan, reliably stoic as Johnson, is perfectly fine in his role, but he really needed more from the script to have any chance of properly fleshing out his character. The by-the-numbers plotting means this film, ultimately, is similar to other throwaway sci-fi spectaculars like *The Tomorrow War* (2021), but, hey, *Warriors of Future* still managed to grab my attention as the storyline progressed. Let's find out why…

A sequence within a crumbling tower block, where Tyler & Johnson try to retrieve the gene bullet from a dangling vehicle high up above the ruins, is satisfyingly tense, pulling you into the adventure. Even more exciting and gripping is a chase set piece that follows, with the heroes hurtling along an elevated, deserted highway in an armoured truck, pursued by rogue military robots. Lots of ordnance is fired and lots of stuff gets wrecked! This is a high-octane burst of kinetic, tough, computer game-like sci-fi action; when all the cluster bombs and bullets are used up, the combatants resort to fighting with axes, knives and even a car door! Ticking clocks are also used well, with characters always on the back foot as they race against time to reach their goals before the next storm arrives and the entire area gets bombed to smithereens.

The film boasts some very cool hardware; everything from the Air Combat Unit's Orca aircraft, the nifty, powered exo-suits with in-helmet comm systems, and a walking robo-tank that's reminiscent of a similar machine in *Ghost in the Shell* (1995).

The script is nothing to write home about, but this is a thrilling, big-scale Hong Kong sci-fi crowd-pleaser. Bug-monsters, explosions, utterly huge extraterrestrial tendrils, rocket launchers, robots, mass property destruction and slo-mo future combat: what's not to like?!

SPACE SWEEPERS (2021)

Starring Song Joong-ki, Kim Tae-ri, Jin Sun-Kyu, Yoo Hai-Jin, Richard Armitage, Park Ye-rin, Nas Brown
Written by Jo Sung-Hee
Directed by Jo Sung-Hee
Produced by Jason Yu, Kim Su-Jin, Yun In-Beom
Bidangil Pictures

In 2092 the motley crew of a spacecraft, that earns money by clearing away debris from Earth's orbit, comes into possession of a robot girl that the authorities claim has a hydrogen bomb inside her. When the space sweepers decide to make some money by selling the robot to the highest bidder, they eventually discover that she's a real girl who has a symbiosis with nanobots… and could be proof that the dying, polluted Earth can be saved. But Sullivan, the dastardly CEO of UTS Resource, wants to annihilate the Earth so that he can focus all his efforts on terraforming Mars and making himself the messiah-like leader of this new eden.

Space Sweepers is a South Korean sci-fi movie with likeable characters, crisp, top-notch special effects, and solid production design courtesy of Jang Geun-young. The near-Earth orbit scenes really look good, and there's enough detail and obstacles to keep the plot interesting.

Park Ye-rin, as the nanobot-enhanced tyke Kot-nim, is cute & appealing, giving the film its heart as the story sees her winning over Captain Jang, Bubs the robot, Mr Park and Kim Tae-ho, who are the initially hard-nosed and penniless crew of the sweeper vessel Victory. As the foursome begin to care more and more for Kot-nim, we start to care more for the characters, ensuring that we're behind them all the way as they combat Space Guards (who all wear stonkingly cool armoured gear) and take part in a battle between multiple space sweeper craft and swarms of attack drones. Just like the Hong Kong flick *Warriors of Future* (2022), this movie has a main character who is lumbered with a grieving-a-dead-child backstory, but here the flashbacks are more affecting and touching, perhaps because the plot point fits organically into this particular tale, which, after all, is centred around the plight of little Kot-nim.

Richard Armitage is a good villain, playing Sullivan as an unbalanced, driven psycho CEO who is prepared to nuke a massive orbiting space factory so that he can both destroy Kot-nim and send the factory plunging into Earth to cause horrendous loss of life. Song Joong-ki, as Kim Tae-ho, also stands out, as the crew member who is the last to fall for Kot-nim's charms.

Managing to avoid being too mawkish or sentimental most of the time, *Space Sweepers* has colourful-yet-realistic CGI that is far superior compared to effects seen in similar, contemporary Chinese sci-fi films. *Space Sweepers* always looks good… and it even uses fart humour well!

TUMBBAD (2018)

Starring Sohum Shah, Jyoti Malshe, Anita Date-Kelkar, Ronjini Chakraborty, Deepak Damie
Written by Mitesh Shah, Adesh Prasad, Rahi Anil Barve, Anand Gandhi
Directed by Rahi Anil Barve, Anand Ghandi, Adesh Prasad
Produced by Aanand L. Rai, Mukesh Shah, Sohum Shah, Amita Shah

This Hindi language period-set horror film was directed by Rahi Anil Barve, with Anand Gandhi serving as the additional creative director and Adesh Prasad also co-directing. It starts by telling the legend of the Goddess of Plenty and her favourite offspring - Hastar. The reason that nobody has heard of Hastar, it is revealed, is due to the fact he was stricken from history.

Hastar, it turns out, physically exists in our world, trapped in a subterranean 'womb room' beneath a derelict mansion. The protagonist figures out a way to get a steady supply of gold from this deity, but there may be consequences...

This is a great-looking, well-told Indian horror tale, full of cool ideas and visuals. For instance, there's a possessed, undead grandmother who has spikes jammed through her face to stop her opening her jaw wide enough to eat anyone – and many years later she is rediscovered with a tree growing out of her rotting-yet-living body!

The idea that an organic chamber beneath the mansion's old well is actually the womb of the mother goddess is an intriguing concept, as is the crown-wearing, red-skinned Hastar, who is eternally hungry for flour!

The way Vinayak (Shah), the lead character, gets hold of Hastar's gold is nicely done: he knows that Hastar is continually ravenous, desiring flour, so Vinayak climbs down a long rope and uses dolls made from dough to lure Hastar into the centre of the goddess's womb. Then, while Hastar is distracted by the dough-doll, Vinayak snatches at Hastar's loincloth containing the gold, causing coins to spill from it. Vinayak regularly repeats this procedure to maintain a constant flow of stolen coins to make his fortune.

However, when more than one dough-doll is used at the same time, the situation becomes much more dangerous...

The cinematography is a joy, the mood is well maintained, with the film coming across as a dark cautionary horror tale. *Tumbbad* is a marvellous reminder to always be on the lookout for horror and fantasy stories from all around the world. When you do, you will increase your chances of discovering terrific treasures like this movie.

A victim is trapped within the fleshy wall of the womb-room

HISSS (2010)

Starring Mallika Sherawat, Irrfan Khan, Jeff Doucette, Divya Dutta, Raman Trikha
Written by Jennifer Lynch, Gulfam Khan
Directed by Jennifer Lynch
Produced by Will Keenan, Govind Menon, Vikram Singh

A villainous westerner steals the snake lover of a Nagin (an Indian snake deity) so that she will follow him back to the city. The Nagin, which transforms into the shape of a beautiful woman, sets out for revenge...

Hisss was directed by Jennifer Chambers Lynch, the daughter of David Lynch, but she disowned the film when it was completed without her involvement. According to Jennifer, the movie that she wanted to make was a love story, but it eventually took the shape of a horror film after the producers took creative control of it. The movie was shot simultaneously in English and Hindi.

Was *Hisss* so bad it had to be disowned by Jennifer? Hell, no – I think this English/Hindi movie is certainly a bit cheesy, but it is also an enjoyable watch.

The transformation scenes are damn fun, using a mix of make-up, prosthetics, animatronics and some subpar CGI. There's a nice touch during one shape-changing sequence where we see the eye slide horizontally across the creature's face. In an early transformation, set in the muddy

jungle, the snake turns into a kind of cocoon, from which its female human form emerges.

There's an exciting sequence involving a chase on foot through the city backstreets to look out for, plus there's even a brief Bollywood-style song and dance moment!

Hisss has one visual that will definitely stick in the memory: after swallowing one victim whole, we see the half woman/half snake Nagin lying on her bed, digesting her meal that has a distended her reptilian belly!

The late, always-reliable Irrfan Khan plays the cop lead and sex symbol Mallika Sherawat is the serpent woman, who has a love scene towards the end of the film, in which she is in human form as she caresses her cobra love... so, as you'd expect, there's lots of tongue action here!

Robert (*From Dusk Till Dawn*) Kurtzman is the creature makeup effects designer, so the overall snake-woman-critter concept is really rather good, so give this film a go!

ASHIAP MAN (2022)

Starring Atta Halilintar, Aurel Hermansyah, Nasya Marcella, Gritte Agatha, Yudha Keling
Written by Cassandra Massardi
Directed by Atta Halilintar, Herdanius Larobu
StarVision Plus

Zul is an optimistic, normal guy living in a poor neighbourhood, who really wishes he was a superhero. He tries to do good all the time and, with the help of his friends Diana & Jon, even films some online clips of himself that make him look like he really does have powers. When a devious property developer attempts to buy up the village and kick out the locals, Zul intervenes, aided by tough rich girl Kiara, Diana, Jon and the villagers.

This Indonesian film has characters like DP Man, who wears a sort of metal eyepatch that isn't really an eyepatch, smarmy bad boy Nico, whose father owns Gersang Corp and wants to evict the villagers, plus nice local girl Aisyah, who runs a shelter for orphans. None of these people, or Zul, have any kind of heightened powers, so it seems *Ashiap Man* will not actually be a bonafide superhero movie, but then, during the action finale, Nico's evil dad injects himself with 'superhero serum' and becomes a red-eyed, powered-up supervillain! Zul, dressed in black leather gear, still manages to beat the hulked-out big boss, the village is saved, and even Nico switches sides to become a nice guy.

Ashiap Man is an amiable, competently shot, kid-friendly flick with a cameo by Yayan (*The Raid*) Ruhian, some unspectacular fight scenes, and a plot which slightly reminds me of a Norman Wisdom movie, *One Good Turn*, in that it focuses on a well-meaning underdog character who is determined to take on an elitist, arrogant chairman antagonist, and is loved by orphans and a wholesome, pretty girl next door type.

GHOST OF MAE NAK (2005)

Starring Nida Patcharaveerapong, Siwat Chotchaicharin, Porntip Papanai, Jaran Ngamdee, Kowit Wattanakul, Meesak Nakarat, Nirun Changklang, Wattana Koomkrong
Written by Mark Duffield
Directed by Mark Duffield
Produced by Siamrus Lauhasukkasame, Wachara Tantranont, Tom Waller

This guy is going to die in a most spectacular fashion...

A young, engaged couple, Mak and Nak, eagerly purchases an old house in the Phra Khanong area in Bangkok. The building is in need of lots of repairs, but with the help of their friends they start knocking the house into shape. All should be fine, but Mak continues to have creepy nightmares involving a spectre-like woman, which he tries to ignore as he concentrates on the upcoming wedding. Soon after tying the knot the couple begin to face mounting problems, including having all of their possessions stolen by a pair of petty thieves, the continued presence of the ghost, and then a hit-and-run incident occurs, putting Mak into a coma. After a cryptic message from the comatose Mak, the distraught Nak realises that she must solve the mystery of the legendary ghost Mae Nak to save her husband...

Using a Thai legend as its jumping off point, this film heightens the enjoyment factor by melding J-Horror ghost imagery with a few set piece deaths reminiscent of the kind of demises seen in *The Omen* or *Final Destination* series.

British director Mark Duffield, who wrote the script too, makes sure the characters that get bumped off are scuzzy, sleazy, disreputable types, so the audience is definitely fully behind seeing the corrupt estate agent get decapitated on a train, a thief burst into flames on a street vendor's barbecue stall and, best of all, a seedy housekeeper become a bisected corpse after a freak accident! This latter death scene is a real showstopper, treating us to a gore-tastic sequence that involves a near-collision with a bus that causes workmen to drop dangling panes of glass... resulting in one glass sheet slicing the housekeeper straight down the middle, from head to groin! One half of his corpse flops to the floor, perfectly displaying his anatomical details within. This is such a gloriously over the top example of practical effects! It's worth the price of admission alone!

As Nak learns more about the legend surrounding her namesake, she finds out that Mae Nak was a pregnant woman living during a time of war. Mae Nak had died in childbirth, but her love for her husband was so overwhelming she returned as a ghost to curse anyone who'd tried to come between them. In order to nullify the vengeful spirit, a high priest had exorcised Mae Nak by

cutting an oval-shaped piece from her corpse's skull, so that he could carve symbols onto it and turn it into a brooch. Now, a hundred years later, Nak realises that the brooch Mak bought for her from a market is that deadly piece of skull!

The ghost of Mae Nak herself is a female spectre with dark hair, a gaping, toothless mouth and an hole in her forehead (caused by the removal of the bone fragment from her skull). If truth be told, she's not much different from the kind of pale-skinned spirits seen in *Ringu* (1998), *A Wicked Ghost* (1999), *Dark Water* (2002), *The Eye* (2002) and *Ju-On: The Grudge* (2002), but Duffield makes sure this familiar element within the horror story is enhanced by including such ingredients as a levitation scene, a death-by-scrap-metal-crushing-machine incident, plus a sequence in a hospital operating room, where a doctor and two nurses are suspended in mid-air by electrical currents discharging from the open mouth of Mae Nak's spirit, which is lying on the gurney where Mak's comatose body should be.

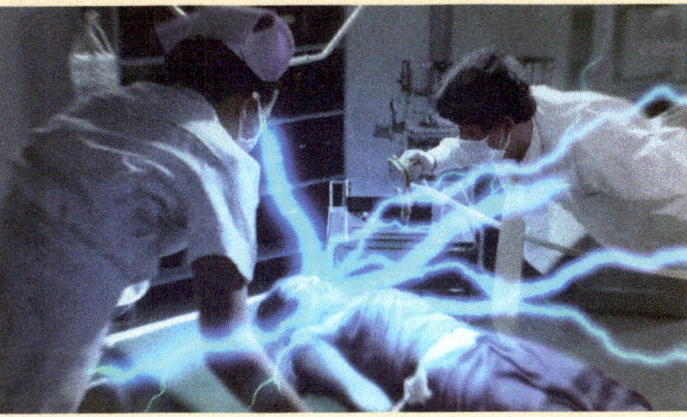

Mak even projectile vomits during this set piece, which manages to give off *Lifeforce* (1985), *The Matrix* (1999) and *The Exorcist* (1973) vibes!

Once Nak is told that an upcoming exorcism at a monastery will be very harmful for Mak, she decides to sneak into the local police morgue, where Mae Nak's remains are currently being kept. Duffield then effectively adds tension by cutting between the build up to the exorcism and Nak's search through the under-lit morgue, guiding the film to a satisfying conclusion, where everything seems to be resolved... but, as I'm sure you will have guessed, there's still another twist in the tale.

Ghost of Mae Nak is a solid and enjoyable Thai production benefitting from the fact its western director ensures the locations have a gritty and lived-in quality to them, eschewing the usual travelogue images of tuk-tuks and pristine temples found in many other Thailand-based movies.

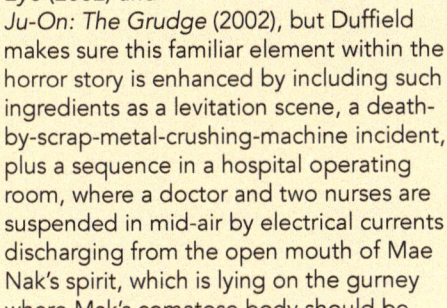

HEADLESS HERO (2002)

Starring Note Chern-Yim, Jaturong Mokjok, Suthep Po-ngam, Natthamonkarn Srinikornchot
Written by Bunthin Thuaykaew, Sommai Lertulan
Directed by Komsan Treepong
Phranakorn Film

Good-looking nice bloke Diew arrives at a village, falls in love, makes some friends, and soon crosses paths with various criminal lowlifes. Diew wins a buffalo race, beats a bad guy called Maad in a kickboxing match and thwarts the robbery of a buddha statue's head... then, during a raging storm, he is decapitated by the vengeful Maad. But this doesn't stop Diew from returning... as a headless hero.

For a chunk of time this horror-comedy from Thailand is content to string together an almost random series of scenes, such as a wizard inadvertently bringing the dead back to life in a graveyard, a bunch of encounters with silly secondary characters, plus many moments of petty thuggery, some monkeys in dresses, a blindfolded kickboxing fight, and smatterings of basic toilet humour. Not a lot of actual plot, then!

But, when Diew eventually goes on his killing spree, the film becomes a heap of fun, as the many villains and their minions get bumped off in different ways, including a scythe in the head, a decapitation by a sheet of corrugated metal, and another thug getting chopped diagonally in half.

Diew rides about atop his undead buffalo, sometimes gripping his detached head in his hands and sometimes placing his cranium back on his neck. His seems unstoppable, until a white-haired, villainous holy man intervenes. Luckily, Diew's wizard friend helps him out by conjuring up four green-skinned ghost midgets!

Headless Hero is a 2002 production, but its photography and lighting makes it look more like a movie from the 1980s, which is not really meant as a criticism. Despite its meandering first half, the film is worth sticking with for the headless antics that grace the screen in the third act.

TOKYO GORE POLICE (2008)

Starring Eihi Shiina, Itsuji Itao, Yukihide Benny, Ikuko Sawada, Shun Sugata
Written by Yoshihiro Nishimura, Kengo Kaji
Directed by Yoshihiro Nishimura
Produced by Yoko Hayama, Yoshinori Chiba, Satoshi Nakamura
Nikkatsu/Tokyo Shock

In a dystopian future Tokyo, where the police department has become privatised and very fascistic, the city is threatened by criminals known as engineers, who are infected with DNA-altering key-shaped tumours, enabling the villains to mutate if their bodies are wounded. Ruka (Shiina), an 'engineer hunter' cop, attempts to deal with these mutant maniacs, but her problems multiply when she has to tackle the police department too, after the Police Commissioner General leads his men on a berserk rampage of wanton killing.

Director Yoshihiro Nishimura, who was also the Special Effects Director, Gore Effects & Creature Designer and Editor, ensures that *Tokyo Gore Police* is over the top throughout. Even the way Ruka gets herself to the highest floor of a building is preposterous: she uses a rocket launcher to fly up there! And then she immediately battles a maniacal engineer with a chainsaw embedded in his mutated arm!

The lead engineer, known as Keyman (Itao), operates sometimes like a black-gloved, giallo-style murderer, skewering a prostitute with hollow tubes, collecting her blood in bottles, then chopping her up and placing her parts neatly in a box, next to her clothing. Keyman later yanks off the top of his own head, revealing an exposed brain and two metal tubes where his eyes should be. From these twin barrels he starts shooting flesh projectiles at Ruka!

Cronenberg-style body horror ensues as Keyman inserts one of the key-tumours into Ruka's arm, causing her forearm to split open lengthways. Ruka, though now an engineer, remains a focused policewoman and is unwavering as she decides to take on the out of control cops led by the Commissioner General, who she finds out was the man who arranged for her father to be assassinated years ago, because he opposed the privatisation of the cops.

Spasms of blood and gore abound, as does extraordinary imagery, including:

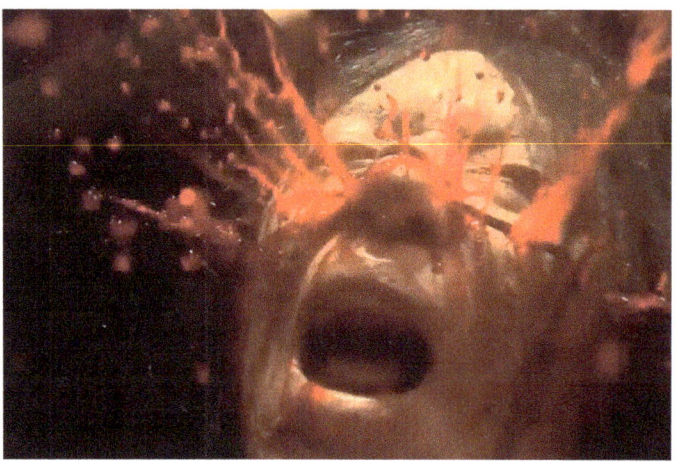

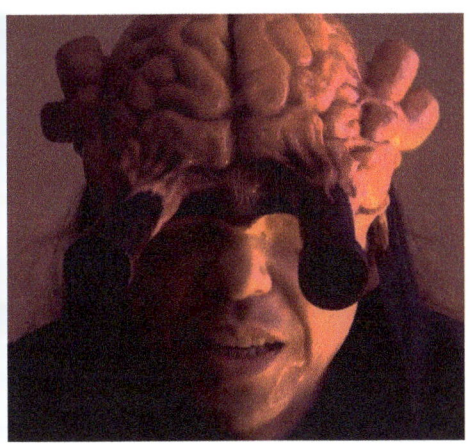

acid-spraying breasts, a living flesh chair that projectile-urinates over a fetish crowd, a shot-up engineer prostitute with a lower half transformed into an enormous pair of reptilian jaws, and an infected policeman's gigantic, red, prehensile mutant phallus that can shoot people! And these aren't the only outrageous elements that this Japanese movie possesses, there's also an amputee gimp woman with katana blades extending from her stumps, a strange, multi-barrelled weapon that fires human hands, and the main cop bad guy who manages to fly through the air thanks to the power of the blood-jets gushing from his leg-stumps!

Eihi Shiina plays it straight as the utterly earnest cop, who continues doing her duty even when one of her hands transforms into a tooth-filled maw and her left eye turns into a multi-orbed fleshy-growth. She really fits the part and always looks great, whether posturing on top of her police cruiser with her gnarly mouth-hand, or when she hacks off the hands of a sexual predator with a sword and casually walks away with her parasol lifted, avoiding the rain of blood gushing from the groper's severed wrists.

The film is told in a more conventional way compared to the director's later release *Helldriver*, but this is still crammed with outrageous visuals, including numerous public advertisements for self-harm, and ultra-gore in abundance.

Tokyo Gore Police is as mad as a box of frogs and glories in its bloody weirdness throughout.

WHITE HAIRED DEVIL LADY (2020)

Starring Zhang Weina, Shi Junzhe, Wang Xi, Wu Dake, Norman Chu
Written by Feng Yuhua, Lin Meiru
Directed by Zhou Tianyu
Produced by Fu Guanjun, Jin Mengling, Ke Jiasheng

Based on Liang Yusheng's fantasy wuxia novel *Baifa Monü Zhuan*, which was also the source material for adaptations including *The Bride with White Hair* (1993), *White Hair Devil Lady* (1980) and *The White Haired Witch of Lunar Kingdom* (2014), this Chinese movie, streamed on Youku, tells the tale of swordswoman Yu Luo Cha (Weina) from Mingyue Village, who is caught up in the machinations of evil Ming Dynasty eunuch Wei (Norman Chu).

Eunuch Wei practices the magic arts of longevity, but now wants to get his hands on a special red pill that allows the Chinese Emperor to continue living through illness. Wei doesn't want to be held responsible for the theft, so he develops an elaborate scheme that involves skilled swordsmen from the East Chamber, the Three Saintesses (who created the red pill) and members of the Wudang Sect, who are instructed to escort the pill to the capital within three days. Wei plans to arrange things so that the Wudang Sect clashes with Yu Luo Cha's group of fighters. When these two clans fight Wei intends to take advantage and purloin the pill.

Yi Hang of the Wudang Sect starts to fall in love with Yu Luo Cha, who he knew from when they were children, but the East Chamber swordsmen Ice Death and Death of Ink, along with Wudang disciple Jun Er, wipe out Yu Luo Cha's village and then spread the rumour that the swordswoman

wishes to bring down the Wudang Sect.

Yu Luo Cha is captured and displayed in front of Wei. She is so intensely angry that her hair goes white and becomes an extendable, prehensile living weapon. Yi Hang, finally realising that brother Jun Er is a traitor, fights him, as Yu Luo Cha tackles Death of Ink and Ice Death. Death of Ink uses teleportation and body duplication tricks to fight the heroine, but she retaliates by using her long locks to ensnare him.

Yi Hang begs Yu Luo Cha to forgive him for doubting her, but she heads off to confront Wei and transfixes the eunuch on her sword and slashes-up his guards, then finishes Wei off. She vanishes, leaving behind her beloved flute, but one year later she returns, visiting Yi Hang atop a mountain, where he plays her flute, full of melancholy. Cue a sad song as the credits role.

White Haired Devil Lady, with its workmanlike wirework, is an okay rendition of the yarn, though it's not in the same league as 1993's *The Bride with White Hair*, which is much more of a visual treat.

But there's stuff to like here, including watching the two East Chamber fighters in action. The black-clad Death of Ink has a penchant for moving about in a swirling, dark cloud and Ice Death comes equipped with a nifty frosted sword.

HELLDRIVER (2010)

Starring Yumiko Hara, Eihi Shiina, Yurei Yanagi, Kazuki Namioka, Kentaro Kishi, Mizuki Kusumi
Written by Daichi Nagisa
Directed by Yoshihiro Nishimura
Produced by Yoshinori Chiba, Hiroyuki Yamada
Nikkatsu/Something Creation

When a strange cloud of ash spreads across northern Japan, creating infected maniacs with horn-like tumours poking from their foreheads, the authorities are forced to build a wall to divide the country and keep their citizens safe. Though the prime minister continually stresses that the zombie-like denizens in the north should still be treated as humans, another member of the government secretly has a young, injured woman called Kika (Hara) turned into an experimental android... who is unleashed up north so that she can start killing off the infected. Kika is more than willing to do this because she wants to hunt down her mother Rikka (Shiina), who is patient zero: she's the person who was hit by an orange meteorite and is symbiotically connected to the alien starfish that controls all of the infected!

This is J-sploitation cinema at its most extreme and bizarre. Amazingly splattery geysers of blood deluge victim after victim, the designs for the zombies are outlandish, colourful and outrageous, crude-yet-cool special effects, which are purposefully stylised sometimes, continually assault the eyes, and the film is madly, urgently, perversely imaginative throughout.

Director Yoshihiro Nishimura, who wrote and edited the movie, as well as doing the character designs, doesn't try to make a film that operates on a real world level: in the reality of this flick Kika can have her heart pulled out by her evil mother and still survive! It's explained that alien goo from the meteorite changed Kika's body chemistry so that she doesn't need a heart, but you get the feeling Nishimura doesn't really care about what would really happen, he just likes the excuse to come up with madcap visuals, including the scene where Rikka triumphantly holds up her daughter's bloody heart and shoves it into the gaping cavity in her own chest!

Somewhat reminiscent of early Peter Jackson gore flicks, this Japanese movie is far more anarchic and surreal. Where else would you see a purple-faced zombie chopping off the heads of other zombies with a big sword, catapulting the mass of still-living heads through the air in a barrage that strikes the vehicle Kika and her companions are driving in? Where else would you see a zombie woman with extra 'child arms' poking from her face and many other arms sprouting from her limbs? Even her legs are actually arms, and a male forearm extends from her groin! Where else would you see Kika's zombie uncle (with a swastika branded on his forehead) chasing the protagonists and collecting a bunch of body parts so that he can construct a bizarre zombie car made from limbs, feet and torsos?!

Some sequences reach a level of utter strangeness that you don't think can be topped... and then an even more odd, imaginative & weird thing occurs, such as when we're confronted by Rikka sitting on top of a massive headless body constructed from the parts of thousands upon thousands of zombies. And yet... it gets even more bizarre and outrageous, as the giant figure grabs two rockets and uses them to propel itself through the sky, with the thousands of zombie parts shifting about, so that the giant figure now resembles a passenger plane made from living corpses! Oh, the madness!

The film fetishises the recurring images of characters getting totally drenched in eruptions of blood, and Nishimura does get crueller sometimes, for instance when he shows one captive young woman getting her nipples bitten off, causing yet another deluge of spurting red stuff.

Lurid shifts in colour, from blues, to greens, to reds, to purples, pinks and

yellows, add to the visual overload, while heavy rock guitars dominate the soundtrack. The movie's credits suddenly appear 48 minutes into the film, just as Japan's prime minister is torn limb from limb in a furious fountain of more blood! Border guards wear implausible, curved helmets, Kika has an engine strapped to her chest that powers her chainsaw-sword, and a female zombie uses her zombie baby as a weapon, swinging it around on its umbilical cord! A bulky zombie dude is covered in samurai swords that poke from his body like metal porcupine quills! The deviant uncle zombie gets chainsawed up the backside and yells, "I dig it! I dig it!" The alien parasite that has wrapped itself around the back of Rikka's head resembles a cyclopean Patrick Star from *SpongeBob SquarePants*, and, well, I can't go on describing all the mega-carnage, creative character concepts and kaleidoscopic chaos in this film any longer!

Just go watch it and see for yourself!

SWORDS DRAWN (2022)

Starring Chen Minghao, Li Jiayi, Jackie Lui Chung-Yin, Tiantian Fan, Yang Shufeng, Bi Xue
Written by Luo Yiwei
Directed by Luo Yiwei
Shanghai Shine Asia Film Culture Media/Yingmei Pictures

When a young swordsman (Minghao) decides to leave a group of powered fighters called the Slevin Sect, the other members attack him, cut off his arm and leave him for dead, but a woman called Xu Yiyi (Jiajyi) finds him, names him Twelve, and looks after him with the help of her family. As the story progresses, Xu finds out that her own mother is really Ran Qingchen, a mystically-powered former member of the Tianshan Sect and her father is actually the warrior Bai Yunfei from Mount Shu. With the Slevin Sect constantly attacking Twelve, and Xu trying to deal with the revelations of what her mother did in the past, the film reaches its climax, in which the evil Sect leader conjures up giant hands, Twelve unleashes clouds of flying swords, and the showdown ends when Twelve creates a super-colossal sword to finish the fight.

Swords Drawn is a CGI-heavy Chinese fantasy wuxia that begins with a battle between Twelve and the other Slevin Sect crew, including the monk-like Straw Dog, who can use forcefields, Burning Tea, who can send smoke-emitting demon masks flying about the place, and Orochi, who can command a giant serpent to do her bidding. This opening fight, which involves the skilled use of loads and loads of flying swords, comes across like an elaborate cutscene from a high-end video game.

Once Twelve loses his arm and is tended-to by Xi and her family, the movie slows a little, as we follow the pretty boy hero as he comes to terms with being disabled and begrudgingly accepts the help of Xi, with whom he forms a romantic bond. But don't go expecting the emotive story beats of a Wang Yu *One-Armed Swordsman* story, here Twelve gets over his anguish fairly quickly... and he even has his missing arm magically regrown by Bai Yunfei later in the story!

Fantasy elements include a large, red-crested stork-like bird referred to as Fat Goose, which loiters about, helpfully pulls the family cart, and fights Orochi's giant snake when the serpent begins to grow new heads, becoming a nine-headed hydra-beast. A fun moment sees Twelve use his guided missile-like swords to slice all the clothing off a local bully.

Swords Drawn lacks the vivacity and panache of Hong Kong golden age fantasy wuxias, but it does try to compensate by cramming the storyline with lashings of super-powered, mystical battles, as the combatants use various magical skills. The horn-headed main villain can turn into flocks of crows to avoid sword-strikes, Twelve's hands glow as he deftly controls multiple CGI swords that zip through the air and form into elaborate formations, and Ran Qingchen uses a quite cool-looking forcefield barrier that resembles cracked ice. These encounters may lack emotional & dramatic weight, but they certainly provide the viewer with non-stop fantasy fighting eye candy.

Ultimately, the relentless, CGI-overload magical skirmishes are this film's raison d'etre, though it's the quieter, sometimes romantic moments, that often work better.

SALLY YEH

SUCCESS HER WAY

By Darren Wheeling

Sally Yeh had a very diverse acting career during one of the most fertile and prolific decades of Hong Kong cinema. From 1980 to 1991 she appeared in 25 films (actually 26, but more on that later), including sci-fi actioner *I Love Maria* (1988) and John Woo's heroic bloodshed classic *The Killer* (1989), with many of them considered classics today. She was and still remains an accomplished singer too, providing, for instance, the theme songs for the superb *A Chinese Ghost Story* (1987) and fantasy flick *A Terra-Cotta Warrior* (1989)...

Although born in Taiwan in 1961, Sally immigrated to Victoria, Canada with her parents when she was four and consequently had a very 'western' upbringing. Her extroverted personality and if-you-want-it-then-go-earn-it attitude would serve her well in the highly competitive world of show business in the years to come. All she needed was someone to give her that first opportunity. She had a natural talent for singing (and some model training as a teen), but feared her Asian looks would hinder her acceptance in the West. She thought maybe she should return to Taiwan after she finished high school to start her career.

But fate wouldn't wait, because during a family visit to Taiwan she was discovered by a film producer while eating out at a restaurant. When opportunity knocks, what do you do? You answer it!

So Sally finished her senior school year via a correspondence course while shooting her first feature film. Her role? A singer, naturally.

Although the resulting film, released in 1980 as *Honest Little Ma*, was not a big hit, it did get her noticed. Her performance of the film's theme song garnered Sally a multi-album contract (resulting in both Mandarin and English records). Though fluent in English from her Canadian schooling and Mandarin from her parents, Sally could not read nor write Chinese very well. To facilitate singing Mandarin she would write out the lyrics in pinyin on large cue cards in the recording studio. This unique process of working served her well for many years.

In 1982, after a meeting with the editor-in-chief of *Cinemart* magazine, she got the local connections needed to start acting in Hong Kong films. The new wave horror/drama *Marianna* (1982) soon followed, seeing her and Chin Han captured by cannibals in a Philippine jungle. Then she played a nightclub singer named Sally in the Johnny Mak-produced *Crimson Street* with Kenny Bee and Melvin Wong.

Marianna (1982)

Film Frenzy Page 36

This was followed by *Golden Queens Commando*, a hellzapoppin' all-female version of *Magnificent Seven/Dirty Dozen* written by Hong Kong's answer to Roger Corman, the cut-and-paste master Godfrey Ho. Sally partners with Brigitte Lin and plays the explosive Dynamite Susie, whose weapon of choice is a stick of TNT & a lit cigarette.

Sally essayed Dynamite again for the equally bonkers semi-sequel *Pink Force Commando*. I say semi because poor Dynamite doesn't survive either film! In a movie with cowboys, Nazi troops, klansmen and super heroines, accurate continuity was obviously far from the minds of the filmmakers. Brigitte Lin also returned for this mission, to lead her ragtag group of femme fatales into the fray of battle.

Note: Jackie Chan appears in the third film in this loose series, *Fantasy Mission Force*, as a favour to Jimmy Wang Yu. And it gloriously features WWII Allied General Abraham Lincoln (!), 1970s muscle cars, ghosts, Nazis (again), along with references to James Bond, Rocky Balboa and Snake Plissken, among other incongruous elements. But, sadly, Dynamite Susie does not return for a third go around (although Brigitte Lin does).

Sally then went on to do a Taiwanese drama, playing Sibelle Hu's sister in *A Flower in the Storm*. The scene where she trashes her room à la *Citizen Kane* is worth the price of admission on its own. Well, truthfully, comparing this movie to Orson Welles' masterpiece is a bit of a stretch, but it's still oddly entertaining seeing her play drunk, smash a guitar and throw a fishbowl.

She did a few small roles, as a physical education teacher in director Yonfan's sexual awakening drama *A Certain Romance*, and as a TV show host in the comedy *Funny Face*, with Eric Tsang.

She had a hit film with the Michael Hui comedy, *Teppanyaki* (released as part of the popular *Mr. Boo* series in Japan). Sally made a more meaningful mark, however, with Tsui Hark's *Shanghai Blues* with Sylvia Chang and Kenny Bee. Her comedic timing really shows onscreen and many consider this her first major artistic performance. After this film she lamented that some critics thought of her as an 'Asian Goldie Hawn'. She seemingly had little interest in exploiting her wide-eyed slapstick persona to any great extent. Her theme song from the film took home the Best Film Music trophy at the prestigious

Marianna (1982)

The Occupant (1984)

arrival in a wet t-shirt riding an orca in 1983's *Just For Fun*. Filmed partly in Ocean Park located in southern HK, this episodic comedy is pure, unadulterated Canto fun from director and star Frankie Chan.

Yeh worked with Richard Kiel, (widely known as the James Bond villain Jaws and Jackie Chan's racing partner in *Cannonball Run II*) in the goofy *Mob Busters* (1985). It's one of the stranger entries in her filmography.

Before director Ringo Lam became famous for his dramatic, violent and dark action films, he co-wrote and directed Sally and Mark Cheng in a fairly light romantic comedy called *Cupid One*, named after the sailboat where much of the story takes place. Although there are hints of

his trademark intensity, particularly in the final reel, the film illustrates Lam's early approach to comedy not seen in

Golden Horse Awards.

In 1984, her music also began to climb the charts with the release of her first Cantonese album. It featured a hit song written by her future husband, actor-singer George Lam.

Sally's first (of three) onscreen collaborations with Chow Yun-Fat was released, the horror/comedy titled *The Occupant*, which saw her play a Canadian college student studying superstitions in Hong Kong, who gets possessed by the spirit of a dead singer. Cue the wind machine, green light and theremin music.

She returned to Taiwan to reunite with Chu Yen-Ping, the director of *Golden Queens Commando*, for a weird dramedy called *Seven Foxes*. Brigitte Lin was asked to open the film with a suggestive *Flashdance*-style dance routine, but she flatly refused. Just not her thing apparently. Then they asked Sally. This was a good move! She performed a scorching intro with silhouetted cartwheels and lots of high-kicking leg work. Brigitte Lin was reportedly not amused, but their friendship endured nonetheless

Actors like to make memorable introductions and Sally definitely liked to make a splash, like she did with her

Sally Yeh, Sam Hui and Roy Chiao in Aces Go Places IV

much of his later work.

The hit songs continued for Sally as she released new albums each year. Many Hong Kong films did not have soundtrack albums, but her albums contained her popular theme songs from *Shanghai Blues*, *Cupid One*, *Peking Opera Blues*, *A Chinese Ghost Story*, *The Killer* and more, becoming best sellers.

Around this time Jackie Chan had completed the US version of *The Protector* (1985) for director James Glickenhaus, but felt it needed some more Hong Kong appeal to have a fighting chance at the Asian box office. He felt Sally Yeh was that appeal, so he added a new subplot and filmed additional scenes with her in Hong Kong. (Note: one of her songs was already featured in the US cut of the film as background music in the bathhouse scene.)

Next she played a woman from the future year 2005, who time-travels back to 1985 in an effort to prevent a man from dying in an explosion (sort of a reversal of her Dynamite Susie role!) This film, *Welcome*, didn't do much at the box office but deserves a wider audience for its themes and unique storyline for a Hong Kong film. It's not an action film and that perhaps hurt it at the local market... but Sally would return to the sparse genre of HK science-fiction a few more times.

Then came a fun role in the fourth instalment of the crowd-pleasing Aces Go Places franchise. In *Aces Go Places IV* (aka *Mad Mission 4: You Never Die Twice*) Yeh reunited with her *Shanghai Blues* co-star Sylvia Chang, her *Cupid One* director, Ringo Lam, and joined two alumni of the *Indiana Jones* series, Roy Chiao and Ronald Lacey. This film shows Ringo edging toward the more gritty films he would soon be known for. The action is hard and fast and the larger budget is well utilised for maximum effect. Cars fly across rooftops, stuntmen flip and fall, Karl Maka does a full body burn, sci-fi visual effects dazzle and, of course, the child actor gets in peril per usual. Sally zip-lines across a freezing New Zealand river and blasts away with a submachine gun in the action-packed finale. Good family fun!

Now we come to the movie that deservedly earned Yeh a Best Actress nomination at the Hong Kong Film Awards... Tsui Hark's bona fide genre-bending classic *Peking Opera Blues* (1986). It's a metaphorical political satire, it's a high-flying action drama with colourful set pieces, it's a French farce-style comedy, it's a women's empowerment film with cultural commentary, and it is usually considered the masterpiece of Hark's considerable career. Sadly, we'll never get to see the original 125 minute cut, as Hark was forced by distributors to trim 20 minutes out so they could get eight showings a day in theatres. The resulting film has such a fast pace the audience feels like it's clinging to the rear bumper of a speeding car just to keep up.

One deleted action sequence from *Peking Opera Blues* featuring Sally

Peking Opera Blues (1986)

not one Hark really wanted to explore, considering the approaching handover of Hong Kong to China.

Gradually, Yeh's film work slowed as her hit records and sold-out concerts increased. Her theme song, Dawn Don't Come, for 1987's sublime *A Chinese Ghost Story* was a huge success.

Collaborations with Tsui Hark continued for Sally. She next had a small role playing a prostitute in a strange comedy with sci-fi elements shot in New York called *The Laser Man* (1988). Hark was a producer on the project, which was directed by Peter Wang (who may be better known to fans of *A Better Tomorrow II* for playing Father Sam). It co-starred Tony Leung Ka-Fai and Marc Hayashi, with cinematography courtesy of Spike doing some graceful acrobatics does remain in the trailer and plays under the end credits. She has stated that Tsui had her jump off a platform into piles of cardboard boxes for fourteen hours until she was nearly in tears. Even though the scene was cut, maybe Hark showcased the cut footage because of all of Sally's hard work to make it.

Peking Opera Blues is one of those rare instances where all the elements of filmmaking mesh together into a mesmerising experience that leaves you wanting more. The ending hinted at a possible sequel, a future reunion of the characters perhaps set during the early days of the Chinese Civil War but, unfortunately, it wasn't to be. Perhaps that story, one that would end with the Chinese Communist Party taking power in 1949, was just

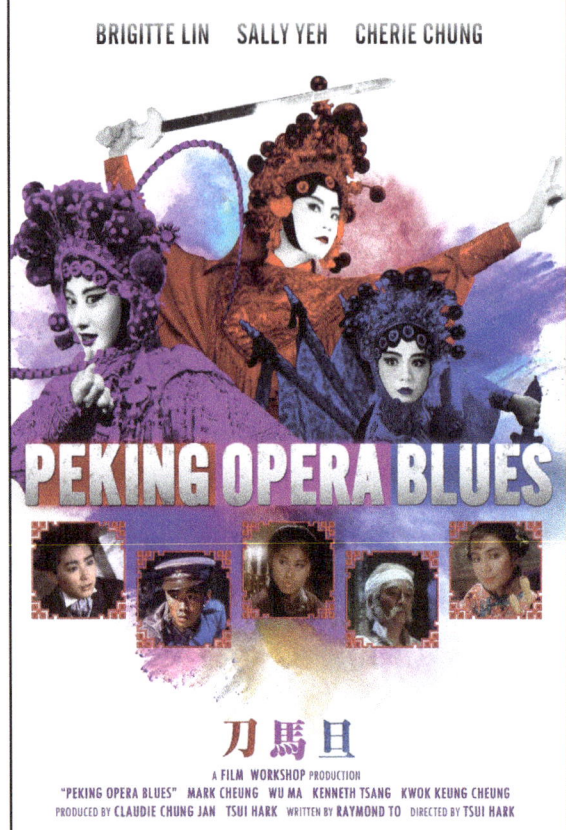

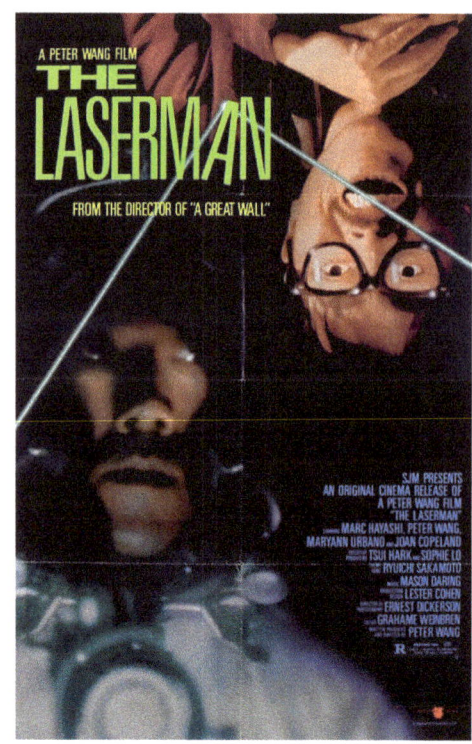

Lee's frequent collaborator, Ernest Dickerson. It's another oddity in her filmography.

She returned to Hong Kong and re-teamed with Hark again for the sci-fi actioner *I Love Maria* (aka *Roboforce*), and co-starred with Tony Leung Chiu-Wai, John Shum and Lam Ching-Ying.

The name Maria is a reference to the female robot in director Fritz Lang's science fiction epic *Metropolis* (1927), which Sally's robot body is designed to resemble. Perhaps to make up for her small role in her previous film, Hark made sure she got plenty of screen time here, as she plays not only a gang villain, but also an evil robot created in her image, as well as a reprogrammed version who helps our heroes out in the end.

If you're a fan of the film, seek out the extended Taiwanese version, which runs 113.5 minutes and features a John Woo cameo, as well as extra fight scenes where Sally's villain gets to kick some more butt. Yeh is not a trained martial artist or ballerina, but is flexible, strong and more than capable of performing convincing screen fighting in the few opportunities she has been given. Strangely, both her fighting scenes in this and *Peking Opera Blues* were cut or limited to the hard-to-find Taiwanese version.

Ultimately, the film underperformed at the local box office, but has since found a solid audience in overseas markets. The colourful, kinetic, effective practical effects and clever filmmaking tricks delight audiences in ways that dated computer graphics fail to do.

Yeh then joined Chow Yun-Fat for the romantic comedy hit *The Diary of a Big Man*, which also featured Joey Wong. The film was goofy lightweight fun, complete with a memorable musical number that'll stick in your head long after viewing.

Sometimes it is the roles that an actor turns down which reveal as much about them as the films they chose to accept. Yeh was offered but declined the role of Rambo's Vietnamese lover in *Rambo: First Blood Part II*. The role was eventually accepted by actress Julia Nickson and the film became a gigantic commercial success. It would have definitely given her a higher profile in Hollywood, but what that may have led to we'll never know. Julia Nickson has had steady acting work ever since, but she certainly never became a household name.

Italian director supreme Bernardo Bertolucci approached Yeh to play John Lone's second wife behind Joan Chen. Second wife? Not the first wife? Sally gave it a

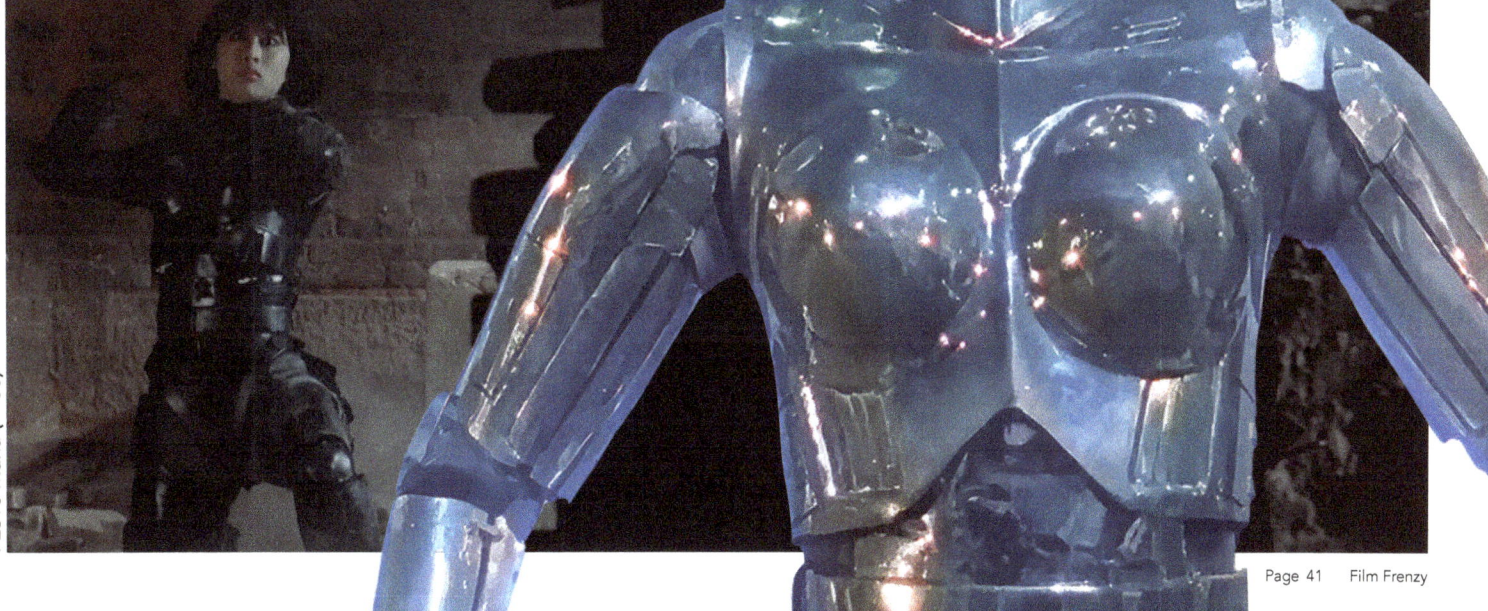

hard pass. Vivian Wu took the role and *The Last Emperor* went on to scoop a Grammy, 3 BAFTA Awards, 4 Golden Globes, 9 David di Donatello Awards and 9 Oscars, including Best Picture, among many others. But if Sally wasn't interested, she followed her heart.

Next Sally was offered a script about a nightclub singer blinded during a backstage gangster shootout. Not another pretty girl for the guys to fawn over in a comedy, or to rescue in an action picture, but a story about her. She accepted, but as John Woo further developed the script, it morphed into *The Killer* (1989). In the end, she was

The Killer (1989)

subtly fawned over and repeatedly saved. Even so, she gave it her all. Sally practiced being blind by manoeuvring around her home in total darkness.

The hit film would eventually go further than any other film to spread her fame in the west. But not so much because of her performance, more because of John Woo's over-the-top action scenes and Chow Yun-Fat's undeniable screen presence and charisma. Her role was ultimately a plot device. A so-called 'flower pot' role. She looked beautiful while screaming for help. Bit by bit, role by role, acting seemed less interesting to her than her music. With her albums and concerts, she had near total control over the final product and her artistic expression could shine through. But films, on the other hand, are highly collaborative works taking on a life of their own beyond an actor's control. Her acting days seemed numbered.

Then King Hu called. Well, more likely, Tsui Hark called, as he was the producer. But the chance to work with such a venerated director as Hu seemed tantalising. However, the film, *Swordsman* (1990), soon became mired in delays, and due to illness (and reportedly creative differences with strong-minded producer Hark) Hu shockingly walked away from the production. Sally, by then, had already completed a few scenes but her window of availability was quickly running out. Tsui Hark, meanwhile, rounded up co-directors Raymond Lee and Ching Siu-Tung when their schedules permitted, and the three of them resumed filming, eventually finishing the troubled production without Hu. But also without Sally. She had to leave because of all her commitments, so that she could properly prepare for her upcoming concert series. Sharla Cheung Man ultimately filled the role. A few shots of an uncredited Sally Yeh actually remain in the film at the 58 minute mark. Because her face is partially obscured behind a veil, the filmmakers did not bother re-filming these shots with Sharla. The movie was a commercial success and spawned two sequels. But Sally was only left further disenchanted with filmmaking.

All the while she was becoming the Queen of Canto Pop on the record charts and concert scene. Some of her hits retained the number one chart position for eight consecutive weeks and stayed in the top 30 for 9 months.

Sally's best-selling Greatest Hits record quickly went multi-platinum. Her theme song for the Tsui Hark-produced *A Terra-Cotta Warrior* was a massive hit upon release of the film. Even her older films were now being released in Japan, which gave her a new following there as well. It was now clear that music was her future and her primary passion.

She agreed to film a cameo in the quickly cobbled together all-star comedy *The Banquet* in 1991. The film was a charity relief project to help raise

The Killer (1989)

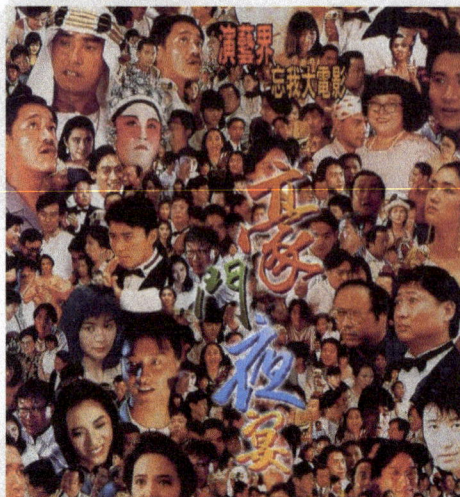

funds for Yangtze River flood victims in mainland China.

This was quickly followed by her final film to date, *Sisters of the World Unite*. It reunited her with old chum Sylvia Chang, who co-directed and co-starred with Yeh (as her sister). The slice of life drama is pleasant enough - it's enjoyable to just spend time around the apartment with Sally and Sylvia like real people. Some nice cameos from Kenny Bee and Johnnie To perk things up now and then but, overall, it feels a little lifeless and by-the-numbers. It also failed to ignite the box office.

The following year Sally filmed an hour long dramatised musical TV special divided into four segments, each with a single guest star. It features Gong Li, George Lam, Alex To and Jackie Chan. Jackie, dressed in *Drunken Master* era clothing, even has a fight scene. This pairing with Sally may have given him the idea for her to appear in his film, *Drunken Master II*. According to Sally, he begged her to return to filmmaking for a small role in his film, but she had made up her mind that she was now fully committed to her music.

Sally's determination to focus on her passion really paid off. The early 1990s music scene belonged to her. She netted award after award... Most Popular Song, Best Music Video, Most Popular Female Artist (four years in a row), even the Hong Kong Artist of the Year award from the Hong Kong Government. She was releasing both Cantonese and Mandarin albums to critical acclaim and multi-platinum sales all over Asia.

Corporate sponsorship deals flooded in. Even her Always Coca-Cola jingle was a major seller. Her bilingual talents enabled her to do English duets with American singers like Tommy Page and James Ingram.

In 1996 she married long-time musical collaborator and friend George Lam, and her output slowed. She'd release 'comeback' albums to great acclaim every few years, and perform concerts worldwide to packed houses.

Because of her Mandarin music and the fact that she still has her beauty, stamina and full voice, Sally is now having a resurgence of popularity in China. A whole new generation of young Chinese fans are discovering (or rediscovering) her work. Sally and Lam both appear regularly on Chinese music programs as guest singers or talent judges. They've done concerts with both orchestras and current pop stars. Her back catalogue has been packaged and repackaged endlessly over the years. Sally has aged with grace and dignity. No plastic surgery or embarrassing cries for attention or cultural relevance. She just spreads her message of love and hope, and fans interact with her through social media as she promotes TAP (Think Act Positive), which is a beneficial spiritual philosophy not too dissimilar to the teachings of Humanistic Buddhism, but without any religious dogma.

She has rightfully earned her place among the giants of popular music in Asia. Sally Yeh remains vibrantly in the hearts and minds of her fans to this day and, looking back on her career both in films and music, she can truly say, through the ups and downs, she did it her way.

MARK DUFFIELD

Interviewed by Ken Miller

REIMAGINING A THAI LEGEND

Ghost of Mae Nak (2005) is a Thai horror film that deserves to be better known, so I decided it was time for a retrospective! And what better way to do that than to interview British director Mark Duffield, who, with the help of De Warrenne Pictures and producer Tom Waller, crafted a Thai-financed, Thai language movie that reworked an old local legend by adding gory set pieces and other cool genre elements...

How did the project come about? Did you already know about the Thailand legend of Mae Nak?

I was originally a cinematographer, working on several feature films, and one of them, called *Butterfly Man*, was shot in Thailand. Over there I got to watch some Thai films and saw how there was a fascination for Thai ghost stories. There was a film that came out at the time called *Nang Nak*. It was quite a well made period piece about the Thai ghost Mae Nak. I saw that film and it clicked a spark in my head, the fact that they'd cut the bone from her forehead, a monk had etched things on it, and then it had got lost over time. So I started to think about what would happen if somebody found that piece of bone? That's what got me interested.

So the legend is well known all over Thailand?

In Thailand she's like Jack the Ripper,

or Dracula... a mythical ghost that people talk about and scare the children with. You know, "If you don't go to bed Mae Nak will come and get you." She's been in Thai culture for a hundred years or so.

Mark visits the Mae Nak shrine

There's even a shrine there, it's amazing. Before we started filming we had to go to the shrine to make an offering, of candles, incense, flowers and so on.

Monks turned up and chanted, it was quite an experience. That was quite fun to do before the film began. It brought everyone together as well, as we all went to the Mae Nak shrine and bonded.

This was your first full length feature film as director. Suddenly you were having to oversee a crew that could include four camera operators, lighting gaffers, tracking and dolly grips, a sound recordist and boom operator, a production designer, props and set dressers, actors, the 1st AD, makeup and costume people, and the script supervisor. That's a lot of folks!

It wasn't too difficult. Thai crews do a lot of high end commercials and music videos, they work quite a lot with international people, so most of them spoke English. So communication was never a problem and, anyway, the language of the movies is quite universal.

Communication aside, the buck stopped with you now as the director. You're the guy that has to make all the decisions for all of these other people.

It's scary stuff when I had to take that leap, but I had to trust in the script - the written document, and trust in the

Page 45 Film Frenzy

casting. You have to remember that I don't speak Thai and this was a Thai language film. I'd written the script in English then translated it, so I had to trust the rhythm of their language, and the people around me to say when things were credible in terms of performance.

You find emotion quite universal with actors and human behaviour, so you just have to go along with it. But it was daunting at first. The film was a six week shoot, so you get used to certain ways of working.

The nice thing is that my crew and the actors saw the director as a key player on the production and respected the director very much, so that helped. I didn't have people trying to better me or anything like that.

Mark with actress Nida Patcharaveerapong

The film has young, good-looking actors and older thespians too, who all play their roles with conviction. How hard or easy was it to cast the film?

It wasn't too bad, as I had Thai people help me and I'd give them ideas on the kind of actors I wanted, and they'd offer me a selection.

I think, you know, the casting did seem to come along fairly easily. There were a few choices where I didn't get my first choice, for some of the supporting actors, but the ones that were selected soon became the characters anyway.

The surprise for me were the two lead actors, playing the young couple Mak and Nak in my film.

They were new, upcoming actors and they were everywhere. You'd go into a Thai newsagents and the actors were on the magazine covers.

I just liked them as good actors and I didn't realise at the time that they were famous. When we were filming in public spaces there would be hundreds of people just watching and I was thinking, 'Oh, wow, they're quite well known here!'

What was it like filming on location in the bustling Bangkok streets? Did you have to get permission?

Yes, you have to get permission. You have to go to the film board and we did have a couple of what you call Thai Film Police with us. It's part of the set-up they have, you have to have certain things put in place, but they do leave you alone and people didn't interfere. I don't think we caused too much disruption, or closed off many streets. It was pretty straightforward.

The heroine meets Mrs Grimm

It was a nice touch having Mrs Grimm, the spiritualist, continually scribbling on a chalkboard during the séance scene. Was this something you came up with in the script, or is this a traditional way of conducting séances in Thailand?

The idea of the séance chalkboard scene originally came from Victorian

A monk featured in a flashback

A thief is burnt alive!

séances where writing on chalkboards was a common practice. I may also have seen it in several ghost story films too and I may have subconsciously copied it.

I liked the image of the cloud of chalk dust over the board. Later in filming, when I had to do a close-up insert shot, I ended up using my own hand holding the chalk.

In the film one of the lowlife thieves gets set alight on a street vendor's barbecue stall. How much preparation was needed before filming this full body burn stunt?

The Thai effects company who did the man-on-fire stunt were brilliant. They had strict safety measures in place and even an ambulance on standby. They probably spent two hours on set preparing everything. We did two full body burns because I felt the first attempt was not dramatic enough. They agreed and wanted to improve on it. As a director, you have to trust the professional team and just give them the time and support to do what needs to be done.

Dried coconut shells were burnt to produce mist and smoke for various scenes. Is this a typical Thai moviemaking method to create these effects?

The dried coconut smoke effects used in the open air scenes was one of the Thai movie-making methods used back then, especially when the area's not built up. We also had professional haze machines in the interior sets, and smoke machines for the exterior Monk scenes.

The flashbacks involving Mae Nak when she was alive were shot at the Kantana Movie Town studios. Does the studio have permanent standing sets of those stilted period buildings that are featured in the scenes?

Kantana Movie Town Studios had a permanent period set back then, as it

A scene filmed at Kantana Movie Town studios

young couple get killed in horrible ways.

I think that's what really works in this film. There are a lot of J-Horror and Hong Kong films that, like your film, have pale-faced, ghostly spirits, but what I liked was that you then merged that kind of story with very inventive death scenes that are from another genre of horror films. The scene with the guy getting cut in half is a gobsmacking, gory practical effects highlight! The company First Ideas did the work, which is so good here. You must have been very happy when you saw the very detailed bisected body they'd built.

Yeah, yeah, I was very impressed. I think having physical effects in front of the camera is always more convincing. There's that element of realism, even though it's fake, that you connect with more when compared to CGI. Even though it's quick and brief, because it's actually there physically, there's something there that links us to it. There's something that makes it real.

There's also the scene of the corrupt estate agent's head getting chopped off, which uses a great-looking severed head model.

Yeah, it was fun. You know, I wrote the scenes not knowing how things were going to be achieved. I was quite naive and just wrote these ideas. I was surprised the funding came within three months. It was quick.

Was it fully funded by Thai companies?

Yeah, it came to about a million dollars.

The film uses rain machines, Tulip and Phoenix crane rigs, lots of extras for the flashbacks, top-notch special effects and so on, and you did all this for one million dollars. Filming in Thailand must have enabled your finances to go further.

Basically you times your budget by five when you shoot in Thailand because you get a lot more for your dollar.

was used in a popular long-running TV series. I was very lucky to have been able to use it. It gave the film a bigger scale and production value. Also, it was easy to get the rain machines in place there.

You wrote the script as well. Did you write it as a spec script, to garner interest in the project?

I wrote the script as a spec. I'd had that spark of an idea about what if a couple found a bone that contained the spirit of Mae Nak? And, at the time, I was also into films like *Final Destination* and *I Know What You Did Last Summer*, all of those kind of 'inventive death' films, and so I thought wouldn't it be great if we included that aspect with Ghost of Mae Nak, where people who try to interfere with the

The crew poses for a photo during the filming of the death scene in which a man is sliced in two!

It helped that the Thai production company managed to get great deals with the FX people.

Where was the FX company First Ideas based?

They were based in Bangkok.

They built a nice-looking animatronic 'death face' bust of Mae Nak for the film, but then the shots featuring it on a train and peering over a grave were cut. Why did you cut those shots?

I think, at the time, I wasn't convinced that it was working. It was one of these times when you have to say, 'Yes, I can put it in but it will jump people out of the film because it might look a bit too rubbery', you know?

The legend of the vengeful ghost of Mae Nak has been the subject of many Thai movies over the years. Thai audiences seem to have an insatiable appetite for watching this creepy yarn as it is told in various ways by different filmmakers...

I think you have to make decisions to show it, but very briefly.

It's frustrating because you want to show things and at the same time, you think if you show too much it will take people out of the film if they think it's a rubber face.

How did you do most of the shots of Mae Nak's ghost?

We had a good actress and used makeup. We spent a lot of time with makeup and lots of floor effects.

How did you film her to give her the wraith-like, ghostly look?

We added some after-effects, like a light haze. This was nearly twenty years ago and CGI was coming in and the companies were keen to push the bar as far as they could. I was very surprised when they did the levitation bit in the operating theatre, where the doctor and the nurses get lifted up. The camera pans around and you can

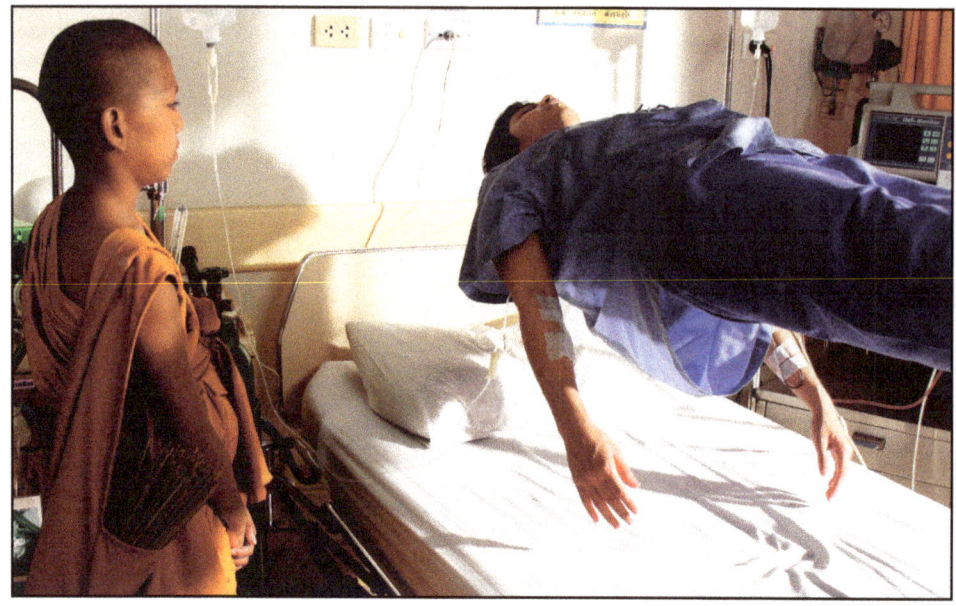

see electricity refractions. I didn't know that they were going to do all that and I thought that's pretty cool.

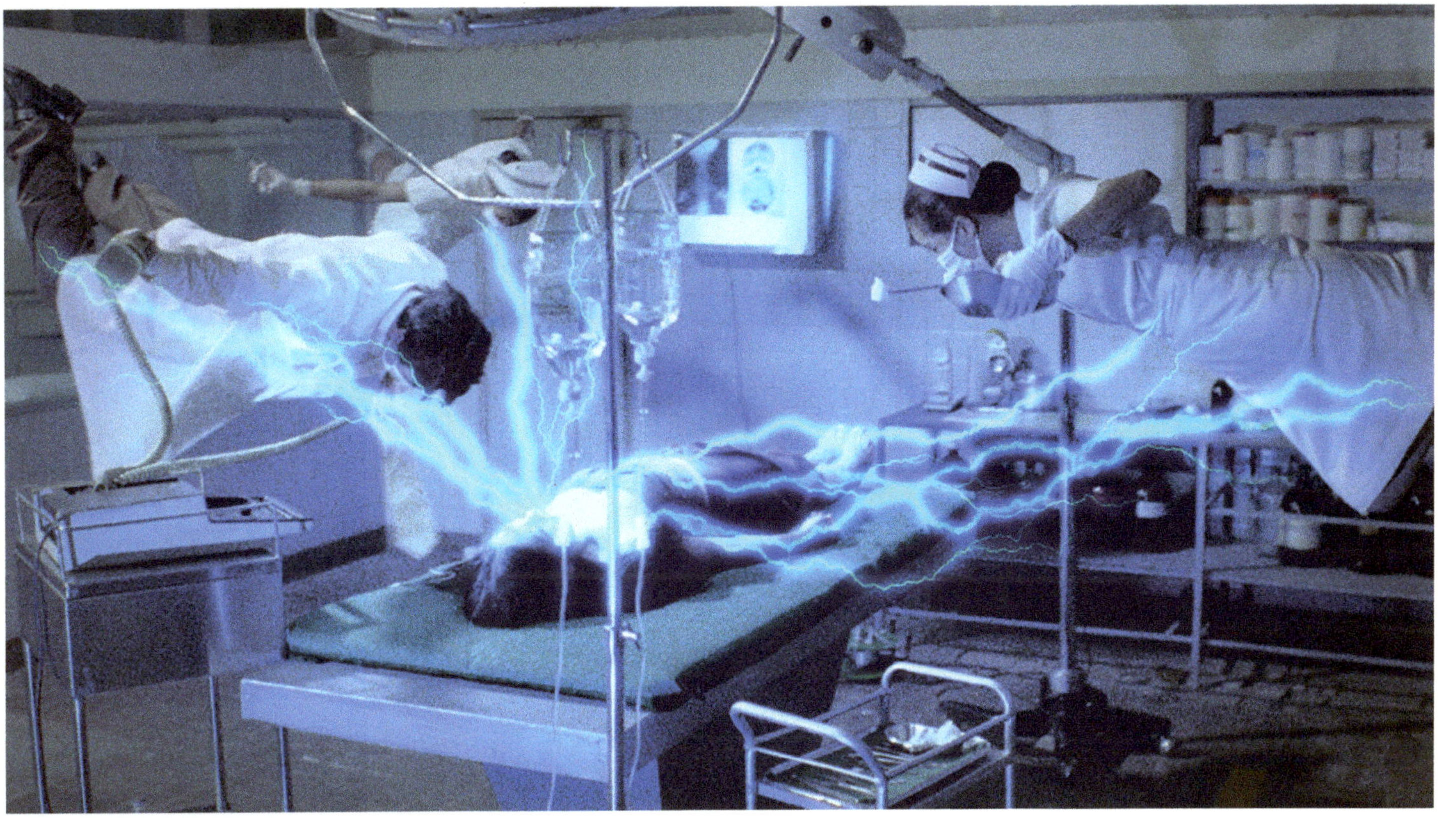

That's a great scene, it has hints of The Matrix and Lifeforce about it, which is one of the moments that gives Ghost of Mae Nak its point of difference, preventing the movie from being just another in a long line of similar Asian ghost films.

It was taking ideas, such as The Matrix-style bullet time effect and putting it in a different environment like the operating theatre. Mixing in the prosthetics and other effects kept the film interesting, making it something you can always watch.

From a script writing point of view, I liked the bit where the heroine has to sneak into the morgue and has to hide, while the morgue attendant talks on his phone, mentioning the new dead bodies that have arrived, including the sliced-in-two victim, the decapitated victim and the burnt alive victim that all died at Mae Nak's hands. Very often in horror films like this you are shown characters getting slaughtered and then they're never mentioned again.

I'm glad you picked up on that. Yeah, you see these things in some films that people then don't talk about afterwards.

Was there ever talk of a follow-up to this movie?

Well, you know, there was talk of remaking it. There was a producer from America, Paul Mason, who's sadly passed away now, who did the remake of The Amityville Horror.

He was very keen to do a remake of Ghost of Mae Nak with an American actress in Thailand. Basically redoing the film but with an American actress.

Like what was done with the remake of The Grudge?

Yeah, exactly. I did a script, had meetings, we talked about it, and then the producer got a bit sidetracked and that was that.

Part of me wanted to do it in America, to reinvent it and base it around witches, so Mae Nak would've been a witch, basically, and the story would have been set around New England.

I did a draft based on that. I thought it could be transposed to America very well. I even tried a version of the script set in Wales, a British version.

Page 51 Film Frenzy

Mark shooting the sci-fi-tinged operating theatre scene

Nida Patcharaveerapong, the lead actress from the first film, tragically died in a boating accident last year, which was very sad, so her character couldn't be brought back for any follow-up film.

Maybe it would have to be reinvented with a new concept, maybe with British characters going to Thailand.

Even without a sequel, Ghost of Mae Nak remains a very entertaining horror yarn.

The film is a nice tribute to the late actress Nida Patcharaveerapong. For me, the film captured her at a key moment in her life and it's nice to keep that memory going.

You need to have made a good film in the first place for people to bother to rewatch it and continue to remember it. You crafted an enjoyable film with lots of novel influences and elements, which is why it will have longevity and Nida Patcharaveerapong will be remembered.

Thank you.

Ghost of Mae Nak was released by Tartan in the USA and UK.

Tartan really liked it. They put it into festivals, so it travelled a bit around the world and I went with it, which was nice.

At the time I was making Ghost of Mae Nak I thought wouldn't it be great if Tartan picked this film up? But it was a kind of distant dream and then it really happened. They were very helpful.

What are you up to now?

I'm London-based and I still write, I'm still chasing the dream, I still have scripts in mind. The biggest problem with all filmmakers is funding, isn't it? Technology is very accessible now, so it's easy to make a film of high quality using equipment that's cheap, but it's still the funding that you need to get things going. But I never stop, I'm always coming up with ideas, I make notes and outlines, and when the time's right I'll make my next film.

I'm still hoping you'll do a sequel to Ghost of Mae Nak.

If I could find the angle, find that spark, to know how to reinvent it, to continue the story, I would.

Film Frenzy Page 52

THE MONSTER ZONE BLOG

Devoted to every kind of movie and TV monster, from King Kong to Godzilla, from hopping vampires to stop-motion dinosaurs, plus fantastic beasts from other media, including books, posters and comics. The Monster Zone Blog, curated by Ken Miller, the author of *The New Essential Guide to Hong Kong Movies* and the editor of *Film Frenzy* magazine, features many Asian creature feature reviews amongst the seething mass of international monster movie write-ups that lurk on the blog site!

https://monsterzone.org

BEASTS FROM THE EAST

In recent years there has been a deluge of creature features pouring out of China. Dragons, giant snakes, mega-spiders, supersized scorpions, killer rats, ape beasts… you name it, these critters have appeared in a bunch of Chinese movies. Some films boast better CGI effects than others, but most of these productions have short running times, so, at the very least, they usually don't outstay their welcome. Many package their stories as adventures, some are just utterly bonkers, and sometimes a monster is inserted into the plot for no logical reason! But, hey, I love monster movies in all shapes and forms, so let's dive into a squirming, wriggling, roaring mass of creature-tastic film reviews…

THE YIN-YANG MASTER: DREAM OF ETERNITY (2020)

Starring Mark Chao, Allen Deng, Wang Ziwen
Written by Guo Jingming, Baku Yumemakura
Directed by Guo Jingming
Hehe Pictures/Shanghai Film Group

This Chinese fantasy flick has a story involving a giant evil snake demon, four masters sent to the Imperial City to awaken stone statue guardians, a killer Hair Demon, an immortal princess, some characters becoming super powered, and magic spells that are similar looking to the magic portals used in the MCU's *Doctor Strange* films.

The film, as you can probably guess from the above summary, possesses an overly convoluted plot. And yet… the film kept me interested, thanks to the evolving, touching friendship between the main characters Qing Ming (Chao) & Bo Ya (Deng), plus it also boasts a decent score. There was, of course, scenes of a giant (and I mean GIANT) snake on the rampage to keep me interested too!

A bit of background info… the source material is *Onmyōji*: a Japanese novel (and short story series) by Baku Yumemakura. Since 1986 it has been adapted as a manga and video game, and was made into two Japanese films, *Onmyoji* (2001)

and *Onmyoji 2* (2003), which were both directed by Yōjirō Takita. *The Yin-Yang Master: Dream of Eternity*, on the other hand, is a 2020 Chinese movie that is based on the novel. And yet another film, *The Yinyang Master*, was released in 2021, which has no connection to this 2020 film, other than it has links to the source novel (and it's actually quite good too!)

CRAZY SPIDER (2021)

Starring Belle, Wang Xusheng, Ren Qing-An, Hong Pu-Yin, Ye Ting, Chen Shengwei, Cui Ying-Er
Written by Tang Ya-Jie
Directed by Ye Zhao-Yi, Tang Ya-Jie
Produced by Ye Zhao-Yi Huang Chuang Xing Yang

Professor Jiang Zhe (Xusheng), a genetic researcher, goes on a mission to Spider Island to save his daughter Yifei (Belle), who has gone missing with the son of Du Yuan Sheng (Qing-An), who is his former boss. Also along for the ride is an armed rescue team, led by captain One Eye (Shengwei), and a doctor of environmental science, Fang Qing (Ying-Er).

Once on Spider Island, Jiang Zhe discovers that the spiders he had experimented on several years earlier have been released on the island by Du Yuan Sheng. These arachnids were genetically altered to ingest plastic waste, but they've continued to mutate, becoming huge monsters with a taste for human flesh! Jiang Zhe must now kick his drinking problem, find Yifei, prevent Du Yuan Sheng from taking any mutant spider eggs back to the mainland, then make sure his daughter gets off the island.

Scriptwriter Tang Ya-Jie, who also co-directed *Crazy Spider* with Ye Zhao-Yi, gives us a simple people-on-a-mission-to-a-monster-island plot, the kind of story I always find fun to watch. Unfortunately, VFX Supervisor Yang Ying's CGI is sub-par.

Creatures encountered during the adventure include a flock of migrating bats, giant arachnids (some can hop like the spiders in *Eight Legged Freaks*) and smaller spiders that swarm about in one scene. The big spiders don't have mandibles... they have mouthfuls of teeth! Oh, and when they roar, they sound like a mix between an elephant and a lion! There's also a giant serpent creature briefly seen at the start of the film. This snake isn't one of the genetic experiments, so I reckon it was included because many recent Chinese monster movies love to feature giant snakes!

One recurring theme in the movie is self-sacrifice, with five characters blowing themselves up with hand grenades to kill some spiders and save their comrades/relatives. Mmmm... don't these characters know how to use hand grenades? Don't they know they can throw these at the spiders, blow the critters up, and still stay alive themselves?!

There's an enjoyable sequence in the movie where the team have to enter a cave system, and there's even a brief moment where the effects actually look okay, because the scene is backlit by the sun. Actually, there are a couple of long shots of the spiders that also look pretty good.

Crazy Spider is a watchable, throwaway Chinese monster action-adventure. Shame the FX, as is often the case, let it down.

SNOW MONSTER (2019)

Starring Wu Juncheng, Zhang Yongxian, Tang Xin, Jiang Yongbo
Written by Sheng Fan Zhang, Pian Jia Leng
Directed by Huang He
Produced by Lin Zhenzhao

Aka *Snow Monster vs. Ice Shark*, this was made for Chinese streaming platform Youku. The story is set in 2045 and sees the Hong Gene Research advance team exploring an unknown Arctic area which, we are informed, has unstable magnetic fields that suggest the zone could produce genetic variations. Contact is lost with the advance team, so Ren Yi Fei (Juncheng) is asked to lead a rescue mission, which he readily accepts to do because his ex-girlfriend, Xiao Qin (Yongxian), is one of the missing researchers.

Ren and his team, which includes chubby motormouth Wen (Xin), Hong Gene Research exec Uncle Lin, beefy dreadlocked dude Tyson and some armed mercenary-types, do *not* begin an arduous trek through snowy landscapes, which is what I expected. Instead, they actually go to a Chinese temple ruin and, after CGI rock spires thrust from the ground, they enter caverns littered with the skeletons of Qi Dynasty soldiers. Here they're assaulted by flocks of jagged-beaked crow-like cave-birds that locate their victims via sound.

Individual birds in this sequence look better than the CGI shots of them swarming around en masse. After tramping through the caves, the rescue team almost immediately reaches a mountainous Arctic region! Either the filmmakers have no real concept of distance, or this quick transition is due to the 'quantum malfunctions' and the 'space rainbow layer hypothesis' that Uncle Lin eagerly talks about for a while.

Passing by the skeleton of a carnivorous dinosaur in the snowy wastes, the team is suddenly attacked by a huge ice shark! At first I assumed the spiky-chinned killer fish had leapt from an unseen lake beneath an ice sheet, but no: this critter actually swims through the snow, in a way similar to the titular creature from the US cheapie *Snow Shark: Ancient Snow Beast* (2011)! Unlike in that film, or *Avalanche Sharks* (2014), the shark in *Snow Monster* looks pretty cool and effective! This leaping shark, which has a mouthful of super-sharp teeth, seems set to devour the team, but a gigantic yeti-like creature grabs the shark, slams it against rocks, then munches on it. This is a dumb-yet-fun sequence!

This seriously huge man-beast is the creature we've come to see! It has ram-like horns and is reminiscent of an enormous, more benign version of the wampa seen in *The Empire Strikes Back* (1980). It seems to be portrayed mainly by a man in a suit, though the bleached-out nature of the snowy landscapes, which are nearly all green screen stage shots, make the white-furred snow monster look quite recessive much of the time, so the creature can be mistaken for a CGI creation even when it isn't.

Anyway, the mega-yeti is friendly, but a scared merc accidentally fires at the snow monster, and the rescue team looks to be in big, big trouble yet again, but a tribe of elf-eared indigenous folk come to help out and it's revealed that their queen can communicate with the snow monster, which is considered to be a sacred animal that the tribe meets on the third day of the twelfth lunar month every year.

The movie's subtle score is quite affecting in places. I'd even go so far as to say that the music sometimes counterbalances the so-so nature of the special effects, making some scenes better than they had any right of being, such as when our heroes and the tribespeople are visited by the humungous snow monster during a key ritual. It's actually rather poignant when Ren and Xia Qin bond with the beast by touching one of its big, black fingernails.

This quiet moment is broken when the mercenaries, led by Uncle Lin, who has revealed that he is, in fact, a dastardly cad called Mr Henry, fire missiles and shoot at the snow monster. The yeti is hit with one of Mr Henry's electrified super-bullets and

falls from view. The mercs then shoot a lot of the tribe and force the queen to lead them to the snow monster, but she takes them instead to a zone full of yet more ice sharks! The sharks get electrocuted, though, and things get ugly when the queen is shot, which enrages the snow monster. The dying queen passes a sacred bangle to her acrobatic warrior-woman daughter Kaya… and then fighter jets arrive!? The planes use magnetic sound waves to subdue the towering yeti, buying time for Mr Henry to shoot the snow beast with another electro-bullet, further entrapping the yeti so that he can hopefully extract gene samples from the creature, which the villain claims will be full of mysterious, useful qualities.

After a finale that comes complete with exploding jets, kung fu scuffles and Mr Henry getting squashed under the yeti's huge hand, the snow monster shares a look with Kaya, acknowledging her as the successor to the dead queen.

As with so many of the tsunami of Chinese-made monster movies recently released, the poster artwork promises more than the film can hope to deliver but, damn it, I ended up enjoying this creature feature anyway, shoddy though it sometimes is in the FX department, mainly because the director managed to inject some heart into the latter stages of the production.

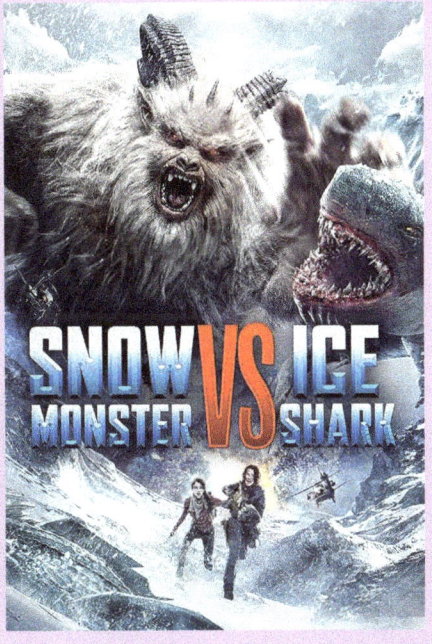

HOPELESS SITUATION (2022)

Starring Liu Yue Tao, Xu Shaoqiang, Lu Shun, Jinqiang Wang
Written by Chi Jianhua
Directed by Chi Jianhua
Fujian Shangwu Culture Communication

During the time of the Republic of China, a band of warriors do their best to stop Japanese occupying forces from stealing ancient Chinese relics. They eventually end up exploring ancient tombs, being attacked by a giant lizard, a long-haired apeman and the reanimated corpse of a concubine. They also fight each other over the treasure they discover and must deal with ancient boobytraps too.

Hopeless Situation is lumbered with a lame title and very artificial-looking digital effects. It also doesn't help that the main group of characters (including a rifleman, a female fighter and a hunchback dude with an eyepatch) are not properly introduced to the viewer, so you're not particularly invested in their plight.

The obstacles these protagonists must face include ninjas, Japanese military bad guys and the aforementioned monsters…

The origin of the huge lizard isn't explained: it's just some big beast that lives in the mountain trails near Craggy Ridge. There are a couple of battles with this (sub-par) CGI reptile, which likes to fling people about, allowing for some kinetic-but-shoddy wirework stunts.

Once the Chinese adventurers reach some caverns they are set upon by a shaggy, acrobatic ape-humanoid with a strange face. This white-furred wild man, portrayed by a stuntman in a creature costume, bounds around the cave walls and beats up some of the people, before he's blown up with dynamite. This is a pretty decent sequence.

The preserved body of a long-dead emperor's concubine becomes the third otherworldly threat when someone foolishly takes a magic sphere from her mouth. She comes back to 'life', her face goes zombie-like, her eyes glow and she zips around the tomb, biting the throats of her victims.

Once the survivors escape from the killer-concubine, they find themselves in grassland beyond the mountains, facing off against the Japanese villains… and then the huge lizard returns for a final fight!

With lots of action, decent comic book-like period costumes and a plot that includes betrayals and riddle-solving, it's a shame that the script is all over the place, the special effects are just not good enough and the dialogue is too expository, preventing this Chinese action-fantasy flick from becoming the diverting adventure romp it had the potential of being.

THE YINGYANG MASTER (2021)

Starring Chen Kun, Zhou Xun, William Chan, Qu Chuxiao
Written by Chang Chia-Lu, Even Jian
Directed by Li Wei-Ran
Produced by Chen Kuo-Fu, Chang Chia-Lu
CKF Pictures

This big scale Chinese fantasy movie, also known as *The Yin Yang Master*, is based on a game called *Onmyoji*, which was itself based on the *Onmyoji* series of novels by Japanese author Baku Yumemakura.

Main character Qing Ming (Kun) is a part-human, part-demon officer (of the Yinyang Bureau) and his duty is to guard demon/monster souls and keep the powerful, supernatural Scale Stone out of the hands of evildoers. He is accused of a crime he didn't commit, is disgraced and so decides to start a new life in a zone where the monsters & demons live.

Qing Ming surrounds himself with friendly monsters who become his familiars, including Kappa-type turtle creatures and some ferrets that can group together to operate a multi-armed costume!

Qing Ming is eventually aided by Boya (Chuxiao) who is, himself, helped by the Red Ghost: a kind of mini Hellboy that grows in size when he is punched. Everything really kicks off when the actual villain is revealed, bad monsters and beings go on the march, and a showdown takes place on the bridge linking the worlds of human and monster.

This film is dripping in tons of CGI (some more effective than others), which viewers may find excessive, but I think it adds to the fantastical tone of this colourful production.

The similar *Yin-Yang Master: Dream of Eternity* (2020) managed to add more

depth and emotion to the main characters' relationships, but this movie possesses a far less convoluted plot and really ramps up the fantasy elements with lots of creatures and vistas.

The Red Ghost is too cartoony (in an attempt to make him cute) for my tastes, but I did REALLY like the monstrous, dark-skinned giant hand that the villain rides around on: with spiked tentacles writhing from its wrist stump, red eyes, long nails

and weird mouth-parts, this huge hand-thing is an extremely novel creation. I loved it!

Give the film a watch: it's a visual feast.

RAT DISASTER (2021)

Starring Xia Yi-Yao, Zhu Ya, Mu Sa, Yin Chao-Te, Zhang Lei
Written by Hou Shuang, Zhang Shengfan
Directed by Lin Zhenzhao
Jiangsu Zhonglele Film/Hubei Changjiang Publishing & Media Group Co.

A doctor called Su Zhenghai (Chao-Te), his young son Yue Sheng and his two grown-up daughters Ting Ting (Yi-Yao) & Ling Ling (Ya) find themselves on a steam train on the verge of being overrun by masses of disease-ridden, murderous rats!

Aka *Junkrat Train* and *Rats on a Train*, this movie is set during the period of the Republic of China and definitely delivers on what its title promises. We don't have to wait too long before swarms of (not-too-hot CGI) rodents start cascading from the carriage roofs, engulfing anyone who is unfortunate enough to be anywhere near them. The survivors rush to the front end of the train (a real steam train is used), only to discover that those who have been bitten and lived are now showing signs of Yersinia infection, a disease which will definitely kill them, but there could be salvation because Su Zhenghai informs everyone that he works for the National Health Administration and he knows that Sulfanilamide medicine, a cure for the disease, is stored at a hospital in the town their train is about to reach. The locomotive stops at the designated station and Su Zhenghai disembarks, leading a small group on a mission to get the medicine, but time is of the essence: the train driver will only wait for two hours and then he'll be forced to leave before nightfall... because the light-hating killer rats will be swarming everywhere once the sun sets.

Entering the rodent-devastated town, the group must traverse a street littered with many corpses and then cross over an alley packed with rats. They finally reach the hospital, which has been trashed by more rats...

The rodent scenes definitely work better in dark locations, where the poor quality of the CGI rats can be obscured by low lighting, such as the sequence involving the characters venturing into the dungeon-like bowels of the wrecked hospital. Here the intrepid team finally finds the medicine in a gloomy, dank storage area, which is also the home of a massive rat's nest. The medicine is grabbed, but the protagonists must run for their lives now, as a tsunami of rats spill from the huge, towering nest. Floods of rats pour from every building like a furry tidal wave as our heroes hurriedly exit the town!

Back at the parked locomotive there's a nicely-handled moment where the old train driver, accepting his fate, begins to sing a melancholy song as his carriage is swamped by vermin. This is a sweet example of how Chinese and Hong Kong movies can unexpectedly switch tone in a story and make the mood-shift work wonderfully.

Doctor Su Zhenghai, played by Yin Chao-Te, remains unwavering throughout, never allowing himself to give up, unlike most of the other characters, finally inspiring the survivors (after his daughter gives an impassioned speech) to join forces and help push a derailed carriage off the train track so that they can escape.

With several scenes of self-sacrifice and the virtues of everyone working for the common good highlighted at the end, this film's message must surely be one that the mainland Chinese authorities

wholeheartedly condone.

Looking past the political box-ticking, though, the film's mix of selflessness and cooperation does work well and adds some poignancy to the finale. And probably only an Asian film would end with a likeable main character getting overwhelmed by ravenous rodents while the camera focuses on flower blossoms in the foreground to create a zen-like moment of sadness.

If you're willing to look past the less-than-stellar rodent special effects, *Rat Disaster* is a solid merging of horror, disaster and animals-on-the-attack movies, with on-the-nose family dramatics also blended into the genre mixture.

NO WAY TO ESCAPE (2021)

Starring Yu Sichu, Xu Dongmei, Wu Youxuan, Chen Yichen, Huang Zhenghao
Written by Lu Yunfei, Liang Zhongfan
Directed by Lu Yunfei
Produced by Chang Bin, Yao Ling, Fu Juan, Wang Lin, Hu Nan
Quanzhi Zhiyan Beijing

Three foxy mercenary women are tasked with acting as bodyguards for young Dr Harwin, who is being sent on a mission, as part of a Special Emergency Response Team, to an underground base called Deep Pit located within the western Gobi Desert. This bunker-building, run by OHM Technologies and the military, is a centre for nuclear materials research, but there's been a gamma ray leak at the bottom of the base, causing the place to be locked down, trapping many researchers inside. After entering the subterranean building it all gets messy when Colonel Krumbach, the leader of the Special Emergency Response Team, orders his troops to start shooting any scientists still surviving in the base, because he doesn't want witnesses as he prepares to unleash a plan for world domination that relies on the use of giant, mutated scorpions!

No Way to Escape seems to be set in some unspecified country that has a diverse ethnic mix within its military, though the good guys do tend to be the Chinese characters. Some of the acting, especially the western dudes playing the obnoxious grunts, is not likely to win any awards. There's an occasional naff FX shot of helicopters at the start (why do helicopters often look ropey in these sort of films?), but the movie has better production values and art direction compared to similar US flicks made by The Asylum and their ilk. This movie also delivers more on-screen CGI monster action compared to its American counterparts. An added bonus is the fact that *No Way to Escape* (like other recent Chinese genre flicks) is a commendably short film. It's definitely no time-waster.

When the soldiers, devoid of empathy, murder every researcher they encounter, you find yourself hoping they will get fragged by the massive scorpions at some point, which does, indeed, start to happen. Yay! The svelte and heroic she-soldiers, called Bijiao, Baizhi & Guiche, obviously end up battling these killer arachnids too, but they're far more skilled and able to deal with these stinger-tailed buggers!

There's definitely stuff to enjoy in *No Way to Escape*. I kinda liked one of the bigger scorpions, which was a CGI creation, of course, but it had a neat, stop-motion jerkiness to its movements sometimes. There's also a nice behavioural touch given to Dr Harwin, who always plays with lego or jigsaws as he works things out, hinting that, perhaps, he's on the spectrum.

Creature-wise, there are several giant scorpions that differ slightly size-wise, plus the occasional swarm of normal-looking, small scorpions that are actually capable of boring their way through human bodies.

The script is forgettable, but a film with action scenes involving Asian Lara Croft wannabes armed with daggers, skirmishing with giant scorpions, is not to be sniffed at, right? These gals are so tough they never seem to consider using guns against these arthropods, they just wanna start slashing the big bugs with their blades! There's one extended fight between these three female furies and a scorpion, deep down in the bunker, that is really rather exciting, as the lethal ladies take turns to jump atop the scorpion to skewer it. They then get in some wirework practice as they're hurled across the chamber by the angry beast!

MOJIN: MYSTERIOUS TREASURE (2020)

Starring Ken Chang, Zhou Xiaochuan, Hu Xueer, He Qiwei, Li Junyao
Written by Lin Jianfeng
Directed by Luo Le
Produced by Michelle Mou

Aka *Candle in the Tomb: Xiangxi Secret*, this tomb-raiding fantasy adventure, based on Zhang Muye's novels, has hero Hu Bayi embark upon a search for what lies beyond Mount Pingshan. There he uncovers subterranean palace-tombs, toxic centipedes that crawl from funeral jars, booby traps, riddles, and a speedy, humungous, six-winged centipede monster.

This production uses the formula that a lot of these films follow: it starts with a full-on action-adventure sequence, replete with danger, exotic locales and a monster, then it cuts back (or forward) in time to a character telling a tale regarding these events.

Mojin: Mysterious Treasure is a by the numbers Chinese adventure that's merely adequate most of the time. It's not as consistently entertaining as others of its ilk, but it DOES showcase a massive, flying, multi-winged centipede with a toothy face... so how could I not give this film a go?!

The CGI is passable, we get the usual digitally-created environments of dark, ancient tomb locales, and the story includes a secondary character who, as is always the case, turns out to be a selfish bad guy willing to murder Hu and his mates so that he

can keep what is discovered all to himself. The villain this time is Joe, played well by Zhou Xiaochuan, who eventually mutates into a lumpy-fleshed monster-man. Joe fights and kills the large centipede-critter, then he meets his own end when he's impaled on a stone throne.

Other Hu Bayi adventure romps include *Chronicles of the Ghostly Tribe* (2015), *Mojin: The Worm Valley* (2018), *The Legend Hunters* (2021), *Mojin: The Lost Legend* (2015) and *The Valley of the Sacred King* (2023).

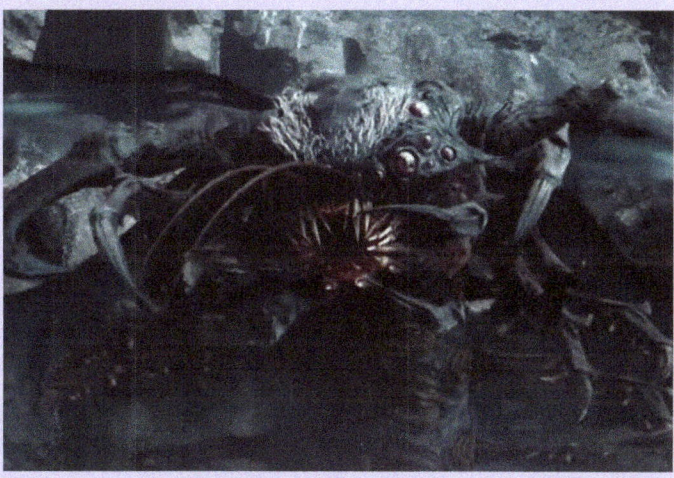

DEEP SEA MUTANT SNAKE (2022)

Starring Zhao Yixin, Li Jiayi, Qiu Shijian, Jiang Yan-Xi, Emir, Waise Lee
Written by Wu Yang, Ma Huai-Chang, Dina Hamiti
Directed by Wu Yang
Culture Media Co/Rabbit Hole Film

A research complex on a remote island, used for genetic experiments on snakes by a company called the Carsi Group, is forcefully shut down by its owner (Waise Lee), who even allows his soldiers to mercilessly gun down the scientists (which also happens in *No Way to Escape*), but (surprise, surprise) some of these scaly lab-modified creatures survive...

Featuring what is probably the most beloved type of monster used in this recent wave of Chinese creature features - a massive snake beast - the film begins on the island, switches to a cruise ship location for the movie's midsection, then returns to the island for the finale.

After multitudes of the normal-sized, aggressive lab snakes, plus a much larger serpent, crawl up onto the ship we are treated to lots of snakes-on-a-cruise-ship hijinks, as a motley bunch of survivors, led by no-nonsense hero Qin (Yixin), dash about the corridors to avoid the slithering killers. Adding to the danger is the truly massive, crested, mutant snake that rises from the sea and wraps itself around the doomed vessel.

Qin and those who've managed to avoid the venomous reptiles escape the ship on an inflatable life raft that drifts to the

Mutant barnacles!

island from which the savage serpents had originated. Here the plot becomes even more monster-tastic, as the characters encounter different types of killer creatures that've mutated thanks to the leakage of chemicals from the abandoned labs. My favourite new critters are giant barnacles that cluster along the shoreline. These can extend long, fleshy, prehensile mouthparts to chow down on victims! Another monster that's encountered is a massive, stilt-legged spider that lurks in the tree canopy and is definitely a rip-off of the very, very similar bamboo forest arachnid seen in *Kong: Skull Island* (2017).

Zhao Yixin plays Qin as a very committed,

serious dude on a mission, though he does get to have a sad, reflective moment as he recalls his dead love, who had died earlier investigating the Carsi Group. Qin and the few survivors are, of course, threatened yet again by the mega-snake, but they devise a plan that ends with the snake falling off a cliff and getting chewed to death by the berserk barnacles!

Despite a misleading title (the mutant snake comes from an island, not the deep sea) and colourful promo illustrations that suggest the lead character will be some kind of gun-toting, super-fighter femme fatale (even though that particular character is killed off near the start of the tale), *Deep Sea Mutant Snake* is still a perfectly fine example of the typical sort of Chinese monster movie currently being created.

THE VALLEY OF THE SACRED KING (2023)

Starring Luo Liqun, Hu Xueer, Zhang Weiwei, Song Jiateng, Scotty Bob Cox
Written by Zhang Muye
Directed by Dai Yilin
Produced by Yang Shuo, Yu Shan
Hangzhou New Studios Pictures

Hu and his grave-robbing adventurer partners are hired by Scott, the leader of the Razer Mercenary Regiment, to guide them through tombs in a jungle country with Cambodian/Thai vibes. Using a scroll map for guidance, they enter the land of the Five Buddhas, encounter various spirits that implore the characters to kill themselves, and reach the throne room of King Xian,

where the legendary Muchen Bead is said to be located.

One of many films and TV shows based on a series of fantasy novels written by Zhang Muye, about Hu Bayi and his tomb robbing partners, this production features lots of cannon-fodder, goggle-wearing footsoldiers, who fall victim to different deadly obstacles, including swarms of tiny fireflies (referred to as mutant bulb worms) that explode if touched, toxic smoke that causes hallucinations, and a gigantic, agile, prehistoric amphibian beast known as the Overlord Salamander.

The Valley of the Sacred King lacks emotional depth (even though there's an attempt to make Hu guilt-ridden because of a dead colleague) and it doesn't really boast any truly riveting moments, but it's a brisk adventure romp with effects that are better than the similar *Hopeless Situation* (2022). Its story is full of riddle-solving, hidden chambers, water-powered ancient devices, massive stone carvings, animal skeletons, collapsing floors, bottomless pits - and it actually starts out a little like a horror movie, as we're shown a jungle temple ritual involving aborted babies used to make 'kumantong' spirits, though this legend of malevolent child guardian ghosts is ultimately revealed to be a hoax.

Maybe there are too many shots of stone discs, sculptures and coffins being rotated to activate hidden doorways, but the Overlord Salamander, with its feather-like gills and red dorsal fin, is worth a watch as it chases around after the characters. It's fun to see a trooper armed with a flamethrower scorching killer fireflies on a rope bridge, and there's also some welcome added conflict when soldiers, infected with blood from splattered fireflies, turn into hard to kill, mindless maniacs with skin rashes on their faces.

Oh, and the film ends bizarrely with an off-colour brownface joke!?

A character falls into the Overlord Salamander's mouth!

THE CYAN DRAGON (2020)

Starring Cui Erkang, Zhang Ruiyao, Su Suxia, Cheng Qi, Zhang Ying, Yin Shaosheng
Written by Liu Jiahong, Wang Runz
Directed by Ji Zhizhong, Tony Wei
Tencent Penguin Pictures

A dying general transfers the power of the Cyan Dragon into the body of Xiang, a lowly footsoldier, who must learn to harness the energy to defeat an enemy nation led by a villain capable of beckoning a massive, multi-headed monster. The general's sister, Ling, tutors Xiang on how to use his powers while they head for the frontline of the war, but Xiang must contend with his instincts to avoid the oncoming danger... and he also starts to fall in love with Ling.

The Cyan Dragon starts with acrobatic *300*-style war scenes, set within green screen-type virtual vistas, that are very cool and exciting to watch, with lots of wirework and characters utilising different powers. This is where we're first introduced to a group of masked bad guys who look great onscreen. They each have their own supernatural skills: one killer leaves a smoke-like black trail as he swiftly moves about, another has a hand that transforms into a swollen lava-fist, and the chief villain is able to summon a hydra-creature from beneath the earth. During this opening skirmish we also get to see how the power of the Cyan Dragon can be used, as the doomed heroic general restructures the material of his sword, causing it to become super-extended, so that he can skewer many adversaries onto his blade at the same time. This battle set piece is great fun and thrilling to watch, so it's a pity that it is the only such large scale fight featured in the movie.

With Xiang becoming the host to the Cyan Dragon energy, the plot takes time to show us how the protagonist is initially rather unheroic, needing warrior woman Ling to keep him on track. Xiang, Ling and a couple of escorts set off on their mission, where they are stalked by the masked dudes, who use a kind of floating, brass spying drone-device to track them.

The ending sees Xiang and Ling fighting the remaining chief villain in a snowy landscape, trying to survive as the baddie briefly subdivides into three different warriors and then expands in size to become a giant fighter with a fiery halo. When Ling is killed by the villain, Xiang screams in anger and sadness, zooms upwards through the clouds, out of Earth's atmosphere, entering the void of space! Then he powers back down to Earth, now dressed as the fully-armoured fighter Cyan Dragon! He mauls the masked chief, but the villain has one ace left up his sleeve, as he summons the many-headed super-beast once again!

This finale, with the totally CGI Cyan Dragon warrior battling the CGI hydra monster in a CGI landscape, is little more than glorified computer game footage, but it's fun to watch nonetheless.

The movie is enjoyable and thrilling in places, with lots of wirework and too-cool-for-school villains. It's a shame, then, that the film is so short. It would've been more satisfying to see Xiang spend time to fully explore the growth of his powers, and the notion that his energy can be personified and interacted with (it leaves his body a couple of times and takes on the form of a small, dragon-creature) should really have been dwelt on longer.

The movie is also known by the title *Blue Dragon of Alien Battlegear*.

MEGA CROCODILE (2019)

Starring Guo Xiwen, Chen Linsheng, Thomas Fiquet, Li Guangbin
Written by Shi Chao
Directed by Fugui
Produced by Zhang Jun
Palm Entertainment

Luo Han (Linsheng), an alcoholic former biologist, leads an expedition to crocodile-infested Hell Island to help a rich businesswoman (Xiwen) search for her missing brother, but it ain't gonna be easy because there's a mega croc on the loose.

There's nothing new here, but I gave the film a watch anyway, as I'm a sucker for exploring-a-monster-infested-island adventure movies.

Mainland Chinese killer critter films are rarely content to feature just the one monster, and *Mega Crocodile* is no exception, giving us the extra bonus of seeing leeches, deadly plants, elephant bugs and regular-sized crocs too. The large man-eating plants, referred to as rafflesia flowers, are a cool diversion: you can't go wrong with fiendish flora, right? The leeches that drop from a cave roof could have provided us with a fun, repugnant scene, but the little, pink CGI leeches are unrealistic and not at all gross. The normal (but very aggressive) CGI crocodiles are shabby-looking whenever they're onscreen, but the 'elephant bugs' did have real potential. These beetles hide in the clothing of an infected female scientist and (so Luo Han claims) are capable of imitating human speech, which is how they were able to make the semi-comatose scientist sound like she was repeatedly calling for "help", to attract more victims to the bugs. This is a compelling concept, but it is not explored. The beetles are immediately fragged with a grenade and that's it for them. The main monster, the titular mega crocodile, suffers from substandard CGI effects, just like the rest of the critters.

This poster does not remotely convey what really happens in the film!

Story-wise, there's a lot of elements used in other, similar killer critter flicks... Secret underground experimental lab? Check. A hero with a drinking problem? Check. Dumb, trigger-happy, cannon-fodder merc-types? Check. A funny, buffoonish secondary character? Check. There's also a plot 'twist' concerning one of the ragged survivors, who is revealed to be a devious expert from the lab who wants to get his hands on the experimental data, a twist which also happens in *Deep Sea Mutant Snake* (2022).

Lapses in logic and plot holes abound: where did all the regular crocs disappear to in the latter part of the film? Where is the poisonous smog that Luo Han keeps talking about? The secret lab only experimented on crocodiles, so what explains the existence of the other lethal plants and creatures? Viewers will probably find themselves not particularly concerned by these questions, because by the end of the movie they will have already forgotten they'd watched it.

WATER MONSTER 2 (2021)

Starring Wang Zhener, Han Dong, Liu Lincheng
Written by Chien Shih-Keng
Directed by Xiang Qiuliang, Xiang Hesheng
Produced by Guo Runze, Jing Wu, Xiang Weibin
Beijing Tmeng Network Technology Co/Hainan Golden Seagull Media

A forensics doctor, Du (Zhener), ventures to a boggy settlement called Shangshui Town to look for her missing brother. The folks here are not too willing to help her, though, because they are in thrall to a superstition involving an aquatic monster they call Lord Water Monkey, whom they fear might punish them if they get involved. Du digs deeper into the mysteries, people continue to get killed, she finds her brother's body, and plans are made to trap the swamp-beast, but things are not as they seem...

This sequel to 2019's *Water Monster*, made by the same directors, tells a different story with different characters, and is a nicely shot and art directed production, using the misty locations effectively.

Central to the enjoyment of *Water Monster 2* is Wang Zhener's performance as the outsider who, after B&W flashbacks, and meetings with various characters, learns that her name is actually Qingling and she originally lived in this town as a girl, involved in a tragic backstory that's inextricably linked to the origins of the monster. Zhener has a well maintained composure about her, playing Qingling/Du as a calm, smart and driven character. She really stands out, especially in a sub-genre where many female leads teeter on being pretty, tough and rather one-dimensional. This film might feature a slimy, leaping marsh monster, but it is obvious that Zhener is totally committed to her role and really shines in every scene.

The town people's ceremonies, aimed at appeasing the water monster, which they regard as a deity, imbue the film with a folk horror atmosphere, while a fast-paced sequence showing the eventual capture of Lord Water Monkey injects some vital energy into the tale. This set piece is full of invention, as Qingling and a group of locals use a series of elaborate boobytraps and other rope & wooden mechanisms to attack the Gollum-esque creature, keep the heroine out of harm's way, and then trap the man-beast.

The story takes an interesting turn, as Qingling uncovers information revealing that the town elders are opium-smuggling gangsters: they're the real culprits behind the ongoing spate of child disappearances and murders! The slimy-skinned, hunched, ridge-backed water 'monster' turns out to be Qinghe, the brother of Qingling, a sibling she'd lost all memories of. Qinghe's grotesque form is, it's explained, due to a

rare hereditary disease, and his feral nature is the result of the vile actions of the elders many years ago. After these revelations, Qingling finally gets to fight back against the bad guys and looks striking as she goes into action, keeping commendably cool, wearing her traditional cheongsam dress and toting a rifle that she's ready and willing to use!

The titular aquatic monster is often CGI in the fast-moving action shots, but he looks much better when a practical creature suit is used, especially during the finale, where we can see Qinghe in more detail. Here the heavily deformed Qinghe is treated in an empathetic manner, as he overcomes his urges to harm his sister, then dies saving child slave opium workers from drowning. It's actually quite a touching ending!

Water Monster 2 is a well-handled, entertaining murder-mystery-creature-feature-drama, so hunt it down if you can, it's worth it.

RISING BOAS IN A GIRL'S SCHOOL (2022)

Starring Zheng Long, Peng Bo, Shi Xuanru, Pang Yong, Cao Tiankai
Written by Xie Wenjun
Directed by Guo Yulong, Xie Wenjun
Produced by Li Shi

A ginormous snake escapes from a snake farm (that'd been using illegal growth hormones in its feed to breed larger reptiles for its snakeskin handbag business) and slinks down to the nearby Haixi Flight Attendant Aviation College, where it runs amok, accompanied by masses of regular-sized, aggressive serpents. A valiant security guard (Long) and a feisty student (Bo) team-up to help a group of survivors holed up in the college buildings live through the ordeal.

This film should really have been called 'Rising Boas in a Flight Attendant Aviation College', but I guess that title was far less punchy! Setting this film in this location does give the directors an excuse to show droves of screaming female students, wearing matching, figure-hugging white skirts and light blue blouses, clattering around in their high heels, as the huge snake rampages about the college, in scenes that really ramp up the movie's cheesy amusement factor. Some girls and their teachers get eaten, then the story transitions into the siege-focused part of the plot.

Despite a title that Freud would have salivated over, the film steers away from showing anything too lascivious, contenting itself with an occasional shot of, say, a small snake slithering from a dead student's skirt or the scene where a snake crawls over an underdressed character whilst she's in the middle of indulging in some blindfolded foreplay with her boyfriend. But none of this is as exploitative as the sweaty promotional art, which seems to promise something more risqué. There's nothing here that reaches the delirious, manic, mondo heights of 80s Hong Kong schlock-fest *Calamity of Snakes*, for instance.

A sequence with the guard hero hanging from cables strung between two buildings, with the mega-snake curled up below him and two smaller snakes making their way along the cables, is well-handled, with special effects that are on a par with the kind of FX seen in similar flicks.

By the midpoint the film tries to become a little more serious, as more people get picked off and squabbles break out amongst the survivors. There's a pause in the action to allow an elitist, selfish student to be lectured about the importance of working people, in a speech bound to please the Chinese Communist Party censors, and then the fun stuff kicks back into gear as the huge snake launches another attack.

The guard protagonist has a moment of self-doubt (heroes in these movies often do), but he's soon taking part in an enjoyable finale that sees the survivors tooling themselves up with homemade fireworks-bazookas. This extended showdown, ending with the recently-eaten security guard somehow surviving and crawling back out of the dead snake's mouth, ensures that this movie remains mindlessly watchable in its own frivolous, trashy way, but it would've been far better if it had retained the silly, kitsch vibe of the first act.

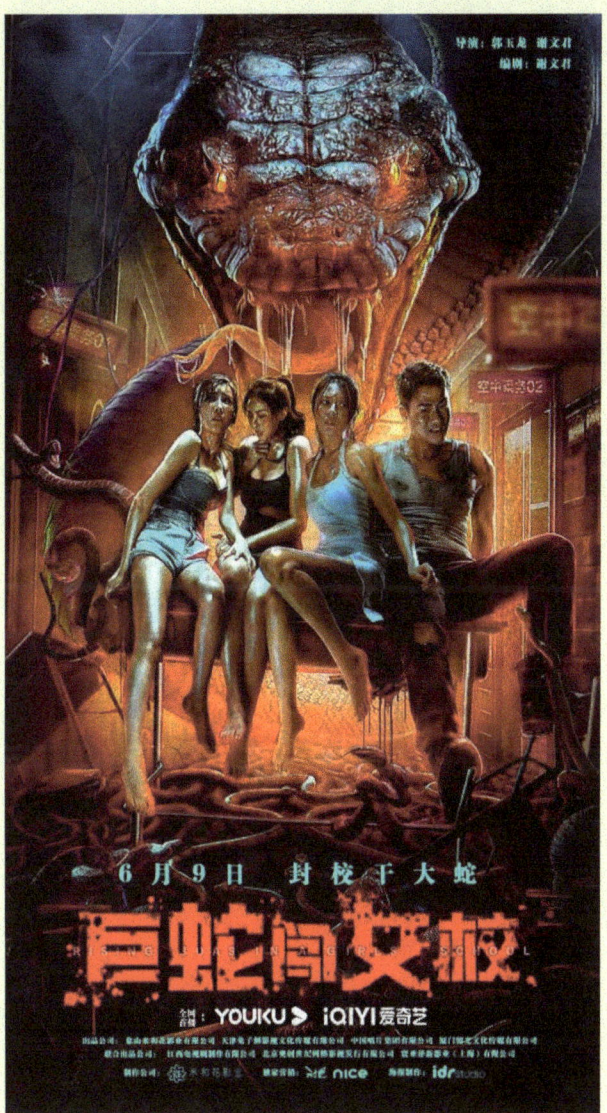

Inspired by Darren Wheeling's utterly wonderful Film Frenzy cover illustration, I decided I really needed to take a look at Asian sci-fi-action flicks featuring high-kicking women warriors. You gotta do what you gotta do, right?

Tough, self-reliant female fighters have been gracing the big screen in Hong Kong for a long time, of course, though these films were within the swordplay/wushu or kung fu genres. Then the girls-with-guns craze gained popularity in the 80s, after the success of movies like *Angel* (1987) and *Yes, Madam!* (1985), but these films usually placed their gun-happy, kick-crazy femme fatales within the real world backdrops of police, crime and action-adventure stories. Even though many wushu films ventured into the realms of fantasy, it's interesting to note that relatively few films during Hong Kong's golden period were actually science fiction-focused productions. But the few that were made are a lot of fun...

The Heroic Trio (1993) has got to be the gold standard Hong Kong sci-fi/comic book-style super-femmes movie. Though the credits say that it was directed by Johnny To, the film has action director Ching Siu-Tung's stylistic fingerprints all over it. This is a prestige, sumptuous genre production dripping with lush lighting, large sets and audacious, over the top action moments, spiced up with humour, violence and lashings of manga aesthetics.

Anita Mui, Michelle Yeoh and Maggie Cheung play heroines Wonder Woman, Invisible Woman and Thief Catcher, in a preposterous yarn about an Evil Master (Yen Shi-Kwan) forcing the Invisible Woman to steal lots of babies in the hope that one will turn out to be the next Emperor of China. Invisible Woman switches sides, after some face-offs with the other two main characters, and the trio clash with the Master and his roaring, bird-eating minion Chan Gau (played by a fit, agile Anthony Wong).

Wonder Woman!
The Heroic Trio (1993)

Listen, I know that in today's world one shouldn't objectify women... but, boy, these three actresses are at their beautiful best here. The late, lovely Anita Mui demands the viewer's attention whenever she's onscreen, playing the most empathetic of the three and looking great in her silver mask. Michelle Yeoh is always a good reason to watch a movie, and here she gets to play both a (blackmailed) associate of the bad guy and also a hero. Maggie Cheung, as Thief

Invisible Woman!
The Heroic Trio (1993)

Catcher, wearing kneepads, small black shorts and stockings, gives her character an irreverent, mouthy attitude at first, but she begins to add more gravitas to her part after being poisoned by needles and suffering from guilt after the accidental death of a baby.

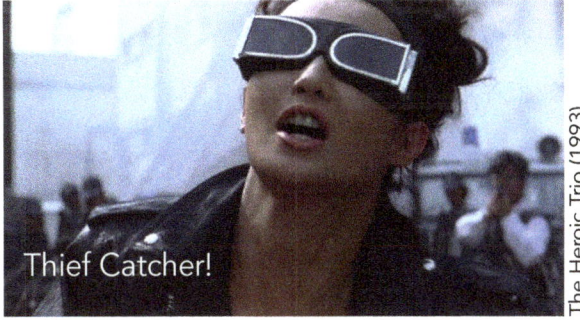
Thief Catcher!
The Heroic Trio (1993)

When I saw this on its release, when Hong Kong films were still at their zenith, it was perhaps easy to take *The Heroic Trio* slightly for granted, but now I appreciate much more the full-on commitment the filmmakers had, as they did their very best to produce a really colourful, kinetic, outrageous entertainment, using all the techniques and skills at their disposal, piling on tons of wirework stunts and practical effects.

The film features some great sets, including the Evil Master's big, subterranean lair beneath the city, where babies lie in numerous bird cages suspended from crisscrossing lengths of chain. There's also a large train station set, which is rigged so that a full-scale train can be slammed through a wall in a standout set piece action scene!

The movie is full of incident and fun visuals: the villainous Master looks evilly resplendent in a grand costume, Chan Gau goes on a killing spree with a flying guillotine, and Wonder Woman's cop husband gets to stoically put his life on the line several times. But the main focus is always on the three heroines, who are willing and able to use throwing weapons, swords, dynamite, and machine guns to beat their enemies!

The Evil Master

The Evil Master becomes a killer skeleton!

The Heroic Trio!

With on-the-nose sentimental scenes that work within the heightened, pulpy world of the story, and a mad finale in which the skeletal corpse of the Evil Master latches onto Invisible Woman by entwining around her with his limbs & ribcage so that he can use her like a human puppet to battle her friends, *The Heroic Trio* may occasionally contain action shots in which you can see the wires, and maybe the Invisible Woman is not invisible very often in the story, but who really cares? This is the kind of production that was made by Hong Kong creatives operating at their peak, something you'll never see again.

The Heroic Trio 2: Executioners (aka *Executioners*) is set later, in a much more downbeat world, after a nuclear explosion has poisoned the local water supply.

Both Johnny To and Ching Siu-Tung are credited as directors this time around, though the visual aesthetics for this film seem to owe much more to To's style, with a moodier colour palette and bursts of violent, heroic bloodshed-style firefights.

The storyline sees various political factions, all with their own agendas that are muddied by secret alliances and schemes, vying for control of the semi-ruined city. Main villain Mr Kim

leader, then disguising himself as spiritual protest leader Chong Hon, which he intends to accomplish by taking Chong Hon's face from its severed head and transplanting it onto his own messed-up visage! Erm, I guess that plan could work...

The heroic trio themselves don't unite until much later in the story. Anita Mui's character has vowed to put super-heroics to the side as she focuses on bringing up her young daughter, then she's imprisoned in a dank cell for a long time, where she's reduced to drinking the blood dripping from a captured mouse to survive! So it's quite a wait before she becomes Wonder Woman once more. Meanwhile, Thief Catcher, now being referred to as Head Hunter, goes on a mission to seek out the source of fresh, drinkable water, so the lethal ladies rarely fight as a unit.

This sequel replaces the comic book flamboyance of its predecessor with a dystopian sci-fi look, and many of its set pieces are treated more seriously, so they tend to have more impact now, such as the well-handled sequence involving the gunning down of Wonder Woman's husband, Commissioner Lau, at a bus station.

There are still comic book type elements, of course, like a bad guy in a wide-brimmed hat who is capable of punching his fist right through a person's body, can wreck iron railings with ease and can punch holes into jeeps. Mr Kim has super-strength too (though how he gained this power isn't explained), plus there's an almost overlooked, outlandish character who helps out Invisible Woman. This dude has a hunch on his back and wears a tatty balaclava. We're never told anything about this helpful minion's background, but we do get to see him shot multiple times in his hump before he's blown to bits by an exploding rocket launcher!

With suicide-by-machine-gun and assassination-by-hand-grenade, *The Heroic Trio 2* is certainly more grim. Even 'nice' characters act ruthlessly in this film, as when the president's helpful deputy (Eddy Ko) guns down nun witnesses, just to keep the fact that the president is still alive a secret. The film's finale, set in a derelict church, ends on more of a downbeat note too, with Mr Kim wrenching off

(Anthony Wong), the mushy-faced owner of the Clear Water Corporation, is behind much of the dirty, corrupt machinations, as he masterminds a bizarre plan that involves killing the prime minister, becoming the next

one of Invisible Woman's arms, then powering his fist straight through her torso. Invisible Woman (who is actually never invisible in this film) responds by blowing herself up with an explosive crossbow bolt, which destroys one of Kim's arms, weakening him so that the remaining two heroines can finish him off by skewering him on an metal chandelier.

Michelle Yeoh became a comic book-style hero once again in *Silver Hawk* (2004), a breezy, throwaway, silly and lightweight sci-fi/super hero actioner that starts as it means to go on, with Yeoh's silver-clad character fighting foes atop a moving truck: she kicks ass and saves pandas!

The plot involves the main villain, Alexander Wolfe, planning to use a groundbreaking AI chip to control the minds of the elite via a new range of ear-phones.

Silver Hawk doesn't have the lush cinematography or inventiveness of earlier sci-fi fantasias, like *The Heroic Trio*, *Saviour of the Soul* or *I Love*

Maria, though it certainly has an icy, cool, shiny look all of its own. There are big, futuristic HQ sets, Luke Goss and Michael Jai White playing bad guys, and multiple high-kicking scraps to enjoy. There's also a self-driving motorbike, a set piece in a large atrium in which Silver Hawk battles multiple adversaries wearing bungee harnesses, and a fight with futuristic rollerblade assailants armed with metallic hockey sticks.

Luke Goss is capable of being compelling when he tries, but here he's all surface image, though he looks as sleek and angular as the silver & chrome architecture surrounding him, so he fits the film well. Let's be honest,

though, the reason we're here is to watch Michelle Yeoh kicking and flipping her way through the film, which she does with panache! Put your brain on hold and enjoy.

Back in 1988 *I Love Maria* (aka *Roboforce*) was unleashed. This flick had special effects courtesy of Cinefex Workshop and action direction by Ching Siu-Tung.

As with *The Heroic Trio*, when I watched this again recently I was really impressed by the film's practical nature: the filmmakers had to come up with inventive solutions to make all the story's outlandish elements work in the pre-CGI 1980s.

The giant robot called Pioneer 1, used by the Hero Gang to help them rob banks, is a solid, marvellous mix of physical full-size props and a man in a big costume. It's a large, red-eyed, clanking, bulky battlebot that can detach its arms and feet to use as rocket-propelled projectiles and has a probe/drone inserted into its chest.

Pioneer 1 looks good onscreen, but looking even better (and the reason this film is being mentioned here) is actress Sally Yeh. She plays both a villainous member of the Hero Gang and Pioneer 2, a shiny she-bot that is bullet-proof, has extendable arms, machine guns in her fists, is super-strong and has a missile housed inside her forearm! She can fly too and, after some reprogramming, becomes one of the good guys.

Yeh is marvellous as the glamorous, emotionless robot: not every actor can win over audiences while keeping their face and voice neutral, but Sally pulls this off, looking both cool and appealing through the film, in a costume inspired by the Maria robot from the 1927 classic *Metropolis*.

I Love Maria also boasts a fresh-faced Tony Leung Chiu-Wai playing an accident-prone reporter, some bouts of violent gunplay & blood squibs, Lam Ching-Ying on a rocket bike, plentiful humour and producers Tsui Hark and John Shum playing likeable supporting characters, but it's definitely Sally Yeh as Maria that sticks in the mind.

Another robot-focused sci-fi actioner with female protagonists was released in 1991... *Robotrix* was a brash, unapologetically in-your-face CAT III production wallowing in scenes of

Robotrix (1991)

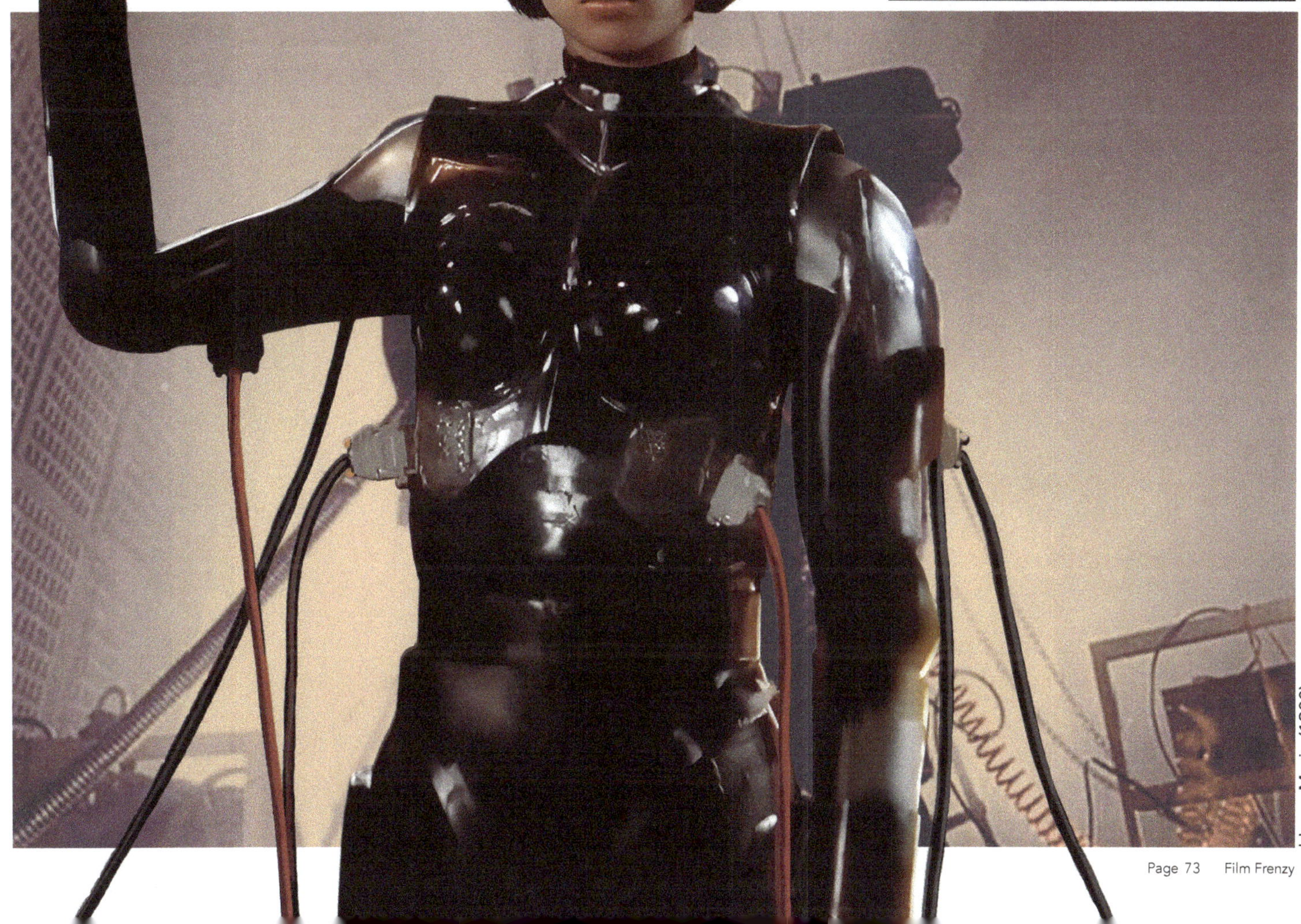

I Love Maria (1988)

nudity, serial killing, sexual violence and fast, fluid fights. But this was all done in a tongue in cheek, goofy way that offset the more salacious and mean-spirited moments.

Starring Category III queen Amy Yip, the film delivered crazy stuff throughout, including detached robot heads, spandex-wearing heroines, cyborg-babes and lots of kung fu showdowns.

Also from 1991 was *Saviour of the Soul*, a film with a vibrant, manga-like feel, with very stylishly-lit sets and fast, kinetic wirework action scenes. Anita Mui plays both a tough city mercenary and her own sister, an inventor of sci-fi gadgets like the 'breathless bullet', which is able to suffocate victims.

Flying draperies used as weapons, pyrotechnics galore, wonderful art direction and a standout prison action sequence, featuring villain Silver Fox (Aaron Kwok) cutting a swathe through multiple guards, belies the fact that *Saviour of the Soul* was shot on a relatively low budget.

Future Cops (1993)

Wong Jing's kitsch flick *Future Cops* (1993) suffers from a flabby, slow middle portion, but it did star a bunch of lead Hong Kong actors playing live action versions of Capcom's Street Fighter II characters. Fantastic femme-wise, it's worth looking out for Chingmy Yau playing Chun-Li and Winnie Lau as Crab Angel.

Other Hong Kong femme fatale flicks that had slight sci-fi elements included Corey Yuen's *So Close* (2002), about slinky computer hacker assassins, starring Shu Qi, Zhao Wei and Karen Mok, *Beyond Hypothermia* (1996), which featured a super-skilled hit-woman, played by Jacklyn Wu, who had a body temperature that was five degrees below normal, and *Black Cat 2*, that focused on the return of Jade Leung's assassin character from the first non-sci-fi *Black Cat* film. Here she has implants that make her act pretty much like a cyborg in a story with science fiction components including power-enhancing radioactive pills used by the bad guys and the heroine's computer-like point-of-view shots.

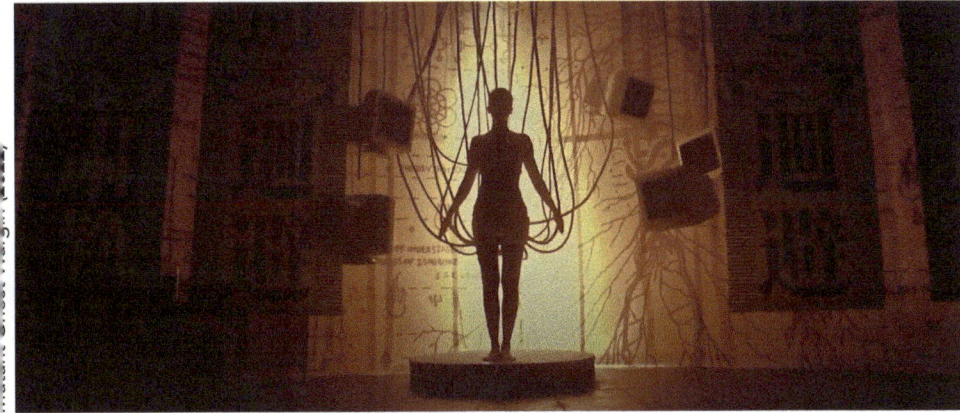

companies know what kind of image sells. Also check out the promo art for *Deep Sea Mutant Snake* (2022), which highlights a gun-firing, black-clad mega-fighter-type babe. She looks great, but in the film itself she actually dies very early in the story!

Since Hong Kong's handover back to China, it should be noted that there are far more movies now coming from the mainland that place tough-cookie female protagonists into science fiction plots. To name but a few, look out for...

Crazy Spider (2021), which features a leather jacket & combat pants-wearing woman protagonist who stabs and lobs grenades at genetically-mutated spiders. She then blows herself up (self-sacrifice is common in modern Chinese genre films) in order to kill off more of the toothy arachnids and save her colleagues.

No Way to Escape (2021) is a sci-fi monster movie that treats us to three fit-and-foxy she-mercs who dress like Lara Croft and love to hack up lab-grown mega-scorpions with their knives.

Mutant Ghost Wargirl (2022) throws future cityscapes, warriors with telekinetic powers, geisha robots and much more into a plot that focuses on a high-kicking, slinky, tough, amnesiac super-gal called Ghost.

Snow Monster (2019) includes a feisty warrior princess and a researcher called Xiao Qin, who is not particularly that tough, but, interestingly, some of the movie's promotional artwork shows Xiao kitted out like another Lara Croft wannabe, so it seems the Chinese

She's a mutated member of the *Tokyo Gore Police*

Robo-geisha (2009)

Meanwhile, Japanese cinema also continues to dabble happily in fighting femme sci-fi action-fests. As with Hong Kong cinema, Japanese films have a long history of productions featuring resilient female protagonists, in martial arts pics like *Sister Street Fighter* (1974), jidaigeki period actioners like the bloody *Lady Snowblood* (1973) and *Azumi* (2003), plus lots of gritty female-led crime and cop flicks like *Zero Woman: Red Handcuffs* (1974). But we're here to talk about mad, magnificent movies where unbalanced sci-fi plotting meets furious fighting femme action, right?

After viewing productions like *The Machine Girl* (2008), *Robo-geisha* (2009) and *Mutant Girls Squad* (2010) you soon see that Japanese cinema not only matches the anything-goes attitude of similar-themed Hong Kong flicks, but they surpass them, at least with regard to their gonzo, gory, often surreal plotting and batshit crazy, very often cheesy set pieces, with many of these films displaying orgies of blood-letting, cruel, creative demises and utterly deranged examples of super-heroics that don't even attempt to ape what could happen in the real world. Let's look at a couple...

Tokyo Gore Police (2008) is set in a future Japan after the police force has been privatised. These fascistic law officers have their hands full dealing with criminals known as engineers, who can mutate bizarrely when wounded, thanks to a key-shaped tumour that has the power to restructure their DNA.

As law and order breaks down more and more, it is left to 'engineer hunter' cop Ruka (Eihi Shiina) to sort things out bloodily. Sporting a white blouse, knee-high boots, long coat, short skirt and a katana, she postures and slashes her way through the story.

Absurd action, spasms of blood & gore, Cronenberg-like body horror, acts of cruelty and mind-jarring scenes of strangeness abound in this Yoshihiro Nishimura-directed tale that sees Ruka become infected by one of the mutant tumours too. But the film ends on a positive note, as Ruka stands in front of her police vehicle, striking a pose with her sword, with a righteous look on her now-mutated face: she might be a mutant now, but she will remain a stoic, take-no-shit law officer too!

Helldriver (2010), also written and directed by Yoshihiro Nishimura, takes place in a post-zombie apocalypse Japan, which has been divided in two by a great wall. All the infected, zombie-like citizens on the north side of the wall, who have glowing, antler-like alien tumours sprouting from their foreheads, like to eat normal humans if they can catch them.

Enter heroine Kika (Yumiko Hara), who has no heart and yet still lives, due to the fact that she ingested some orange alien substance that came down to Earth on a meteorite. A rogue member of the government orders Kika to be turned into Subject 001, an experimental android to be let loose to reduce the number of the infected.

Kika, who is basically an attractive young woman with what looks like a two-stroke engine fitted to her chest, goes on a mission beyond the wall, helped by several other characters.

Armed with a very cool, curved chainsaw-sword, Kika hunts down her mother Rikka (Eihi Shiina) because she's the source of the infection: a psychotic madwoman symbiotically linked to an alien starfish that's wrapped around the back of her head!

Totally bonkers and gory beyond belief, *Helldriver* throws its furious fighting femme into a world of extreme weirdness. With tons of prosthetics and crude-yet-cool-and-stylised FX, this film reaches a crescendo of craziness and depravity that often threatens to short-circuit the viewer's brain... and then, you guessed it, it gets even stranger!

There are other sci-fi-style battling beauty productions out there from all over Asia, of course, and hopefully the movies you've read about here will tempt you to revisit some of them or chase down others you have not yet had the pleasure of viewing.

Go on, you know you want to do it!

HORROR FILMS
POSTER GALLERY
from Hong Kong, Taiwan and Indonesia

The following pages feature a super selection of horror movie posters from the collection of the one and only **Toby Russell**, who is the director of such documentaries as *Death by Misadventure: The Mysterious Life of Bruce Lee* (1993), *Cinema of Vengeance* (1994) and *Top Fighter* (1995). Toby has also acted in a bunch of Hong Kong and Taiwanese films, including the amazingly unhinged *Ninja the Final Duel* (1986). He also played the part of a sailor in *Possessed II* (1984), which has its poster included in this gallery...

Encounters of the Spooky Kind (1980) This Hong Kong favourite from Sammo Hung wonderfully blends kung fu with funny horror hijinks.

The Nine Demons (1984) A weird Hong Kong horror-martial-arts-actioner from director Chang Cheh.

Devil Fetus (1983) This Hong Kong film features a white-haired demon, the eating of a dead dog and a character who splits in two, but it seems the poster wants viewers to think they're about to watch something like *Rosemary's Baby* (1968).

Dead Curse (1985) As this Hong Kong horror tale was a CAT III flick, the designers of this poster definitely decided that lots of bare female skin was the way to go. Note that she has a green face: she must be evil!

The Phantom Killer (1981) A Hong Kong production from Golden Harvest, it starred Wai Pak, who also appeared in *The Devil & the Ghostbuster* (1988), and Chung Fat, who was in other horror movies, including *New Mr Vampire* (1986).

Bloody Wedding (1987) This is a gorgeously-painted poster for an Indonesian horror-actioner that headlined Billy Chong (Willy Dozan), the star of the hugely enjoyable *Kung Fu from Beyond the Grave* (1982).

The Beasts (1980) The poster designer used an impactful graphic design approach to help promote this grim, sleazy Hong Kong revenge-shocker, which was directed by Dennis Yu.

The Boxer's Omen (1983) Colourful montage (VHS sleeve) artwork for a wild Hong Kong horror flick that's loaded with offal, maggots, laser beam effects, eels, nudity, vomit-eating and chanting monks!

The Devil Cat (1992) Poster for a Taiwanese horror film that starred Wong Mei-Suet, who also appeared in the Taiwanese ghost movie *Spirit Love* (1989).

Human Lanterns (1982) Shaw Brothers, who produced this period-set Hong Kong horror story about a mad, murderous lantern maker, made sure the poster for their movie was a stonkingly good one!

Devil Sorcery (1988) Poster for a Hong Kong cheapie about wizards, flying human heads and the puking-up of insects! So... what's not to like?!

Aloha, The Little Vampire (1988) Really nice illustration work on this poster for a Taiwanese production featuring a kid vampire, martial arts and comedy.

The Blue Jean Monster (1991) Poster for a Hong Kong movie that gave the late, great Shing Fui-On the chance to be the lead for once, playing a reanimated dead cop seeking revenge against the Triads!

Possessed II (1984) This Hong Kong horror sequel was made by David Lai, who directed the first *Possessed* film too. Lai also worked on the great flicks *Saviour of the Soul* (1991) and *The Scorpion King* (1992).

Vampire Kid II (1988) A lovely illustration style is used for this poster, for a Taiwanese movie focusing on the antics of a hopping vampire child. Check out that dog next to the vamp!

***Bewitched* (1981)** Maybe the poster is not entirely representative of what actually happens in this very entertaining Hong Kong black magic tale from Shaw Brothers, but it's bloody awesome to look at!

Revenge of the Corpse (1981) And here's another cracking Hong Kong film poster from Shaw Brothers, placing the villain, played by the always reliable Lo Lieh, front and centre.

NEXT ISSUE

KAIJU ALERT!

www.ingramcontent.com/pod-product-compliance
Lightning Source LLC
Chambersburg PA
CBHW061124170426
43209CB00013B/1667